Chiswick House

and

Gardens

A History

Gillian Clegg

McHugh Publications

First published in 2011 by McHugh Publications,
33 Chiswick Staithe, Hartington Road, London W4 3TP
email: gillian.clegg@btinernet.com

ISBN 978-0-9569164-0-2

Page layout: adam.watson@stradivari.net
Cover design: Ken Reilly
Page design: Anne Paton

Printed by MPG-Biddles Ltd,
24 Rollesby Road, Hardwick Industrial Estate,
Kings Lynn, Norfolk PE30 4LS.
www.mpg-biddles.co.uk

Cover illustration:
Detail from
'A View from an elevated position on the terrace looking across
the southern end of the canal to the side of the villa'
by Pieter Andreas Rysbrack (c.1684-1748)
(© Devonshire Collection, Chatsworth.
Reproduced by permission of the
Chatsworth Settlement Trustees)

Chiswick House and Gardens: A History

CONTENTS

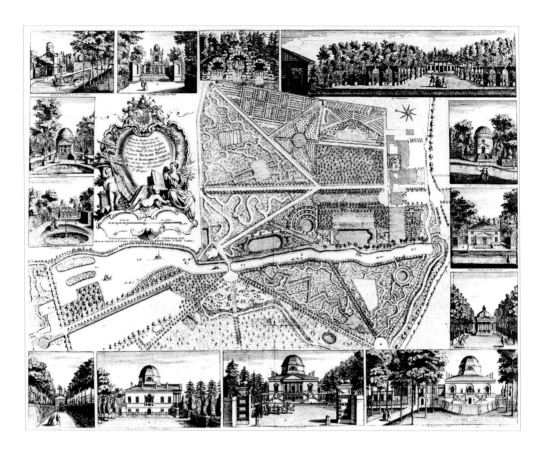

Fig 1. John Rocque's engraved survey of Chiswick, published in 1736. The buildings shown in the boxed drawings are (from left to right): top 1.Bagnio from the rear; 2. Bagnio from the front; 3. Cascade; 4. Orangery and part of the Deer House (this was not the Orangery eventually built). 2nd row: 1. Ionic Temple from the front; Ionic Temple from the rear. 3rd row: 1. the `volerie' (Lady Burlington's flower garden and aviary); 2. the Temple by the Water. 4th row: the Domed Building. 5th row: 1. Rustic House; 2. Chiswick House (side); 3. Chiswick House (front); 4. Chiswick House (rear)
(Local Studies, Chiswick Library)

INTRODUCTION

This is the story of a house with iconic architecture, historically important gardens, and famous inhabitants; a house that was also the scene of some of the most sumptuous parties ever held in the 18th and 19th centuries, before falling on hard times in the 20th century. The house and gardens have now been rescued and are being restored to something approaching their former glory.

Chiswick House was designed by its owner, the 3rd Earl of Burlington known as `the architect earl'. When it was built between 1726 and 1729 it was one of the first and finest examples of a new style of English architecture, neo-Palladianism, which was to dominate building design for the first half of the 18th century and influence it thereafter. Chiswick House is a designated Ancient Monument and is listed Grade I in the Register of Historic Buildings.

The Chiswick House gardens first set a trend for Classical gardens – statuary and buildings interspersed with water and greenery. Then, a few years later, due to the influence of William Kent, the gardens became the birthplace of the English Landscape Movement, a more naturalistic, less formal style of gardening. The gardens are listed Grade I in the Register of Public Parks and Gardens of Historic Interest

Chiswick House was a centre of fashionable and clever society in the 18th and 19th centuries. The best known literary and artistic people of the day, such as Alexander Pope, John Gay, Jonathan Swift and David Garrick regularly visited their friend Lord Burlington, and Whig politicians met and plotted later in the century when the house was home to Lord Burlington's grandson, the 5th Duke of Devonshire and his charismatic wife, Georgiana. Kings, emperors and other notables were entertained in the 19th century at Chiswick by the 6th Duke of Devonshire who hosted some of the most lavish parties ever held in this country. Two eminent politicians – Charles James Fox and George Canning - died in Chiswick House and it was briefly a Royal residence when the Prince of Wales (later Edward VII) rented it from the 7th Duke of Devonshire between 1869 and 1877.

Then began a decline. The house and gardens were used as a mental asylum for 36 years until 1929 when the 9th Duke of Devonshire sold the estate to the Middlesex County Council which leased it to the Brentford and Chiswick Urban District Council. With inadequate funds to maintain a house and gardens of such national historic importance, both the building and its grounds began to deteriorate. The house was saved by being gifted to the nation in 1948 and restored by the Ministry of Works. It was opened to the public in 1958 and is now in the care of English Heritage.

The gardens continued to suffer from neglect for another 50 years until the Chiswick House and Gardens Trust, formed in 2005 to manage both house and

Fig 2. Chiswick House from the garden showing the Link Building to its immediate left and the Summer Parlour beyond (© Adam Watson)

garden, carried out a major regeneration project to restore the gardens with funding from the Heritage Lottery Fund.

This book, written by one of the people compiling an archive for the Chiswick House and Gardens Trust, charts the history of Chiswick House from the building of the first Jacobean mansion in the 17th century through to the completion of the restoration of the gardens in 2010. It contains previously unpublished information on the house's residents and the events that took place there after the death of the 6th Duke of Devonshire. The author is grateful to Pamela Bater for allowing access to her research for the periods 1858 to 1929 and 1940 to 1945. The author is grateful to the Chiswick House and Gardens Trust for allowing her to use material from the archive and to English Heritage for permission to take photographs inside the house.

She would also like to thank Adam Watson who laid out the book; Ken Reilly who designed the cover, Anne Paton who designed the pages and the following people for their different but invaluable help: Sarah Finch-Crisp and Fiona Crumley of the Chiswick House and Gardens Trust, Stuart Band of the Devonshire Archive, Chatsworth; James Marshall and Carolyn Hammond of Local Studies, Chiswick Library, Ricky Pound, Visitor Operations Site Supervisor at Chiswick House; Karen Liebreich, David Best, Simon Francis, Peter Hammond, Juliet Page, William Roe and Shirley Seaton.

Chapter 1

THE JACOBEAN MANSION
AND ITS SURROUNDINGS

Setting the scene

The building of the Palladian villa, known today as Chiswick House, was not begun until 1726. The house that the young Richard Boyle, 3rd Earl of Burlington inherited in Chiswick was a Jacobean mansion in Burlington Lane close to the River Thames (See Fig 6).

In 1704 the place we know as Chiswick (the name means cheese farm) was actually composed of four separate villages —Old Chiswick which nestled around St Nicholas Church and Chiswick Mall; Strand on the Green, a straggling village of fisher folk; a small hamlet called Little Sutton, and Turnham Green which grew up along what was, until the middle of the 20th century, the main road to the west of England, pounded by horses, carts and, later, gaily-painted coaches thundering their way to Bath, Exeter and other places west.

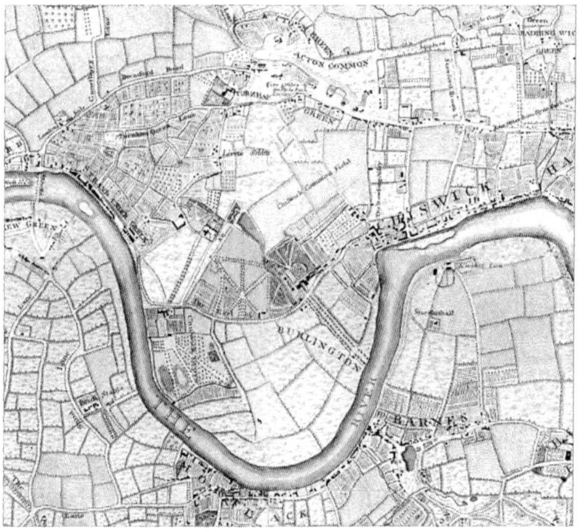

Chiswick had two manors, both belonging to St Paul's Cathedral: the Prebendal manor covered the eastern part of the area with a manor house in Chiswick Mall; Sutton Manor, which owned the western area, had its manor house on what is now the junction of Sutton Court Road with Fauconberg Road.

Fig 3. Chiswick in the middle of the 18th century. The Chiswick House estate is in the centre right with an avenue leading to the Thames. Map by John Rocque (Local Studies, Chiswick Library)

Being generally low lying, Chiswick was quite a wet area. Early maps show it was dotted with ponds, lakes and streams (now underground). There was also a moat which surrounded a one time Royal residence. This was a house built on Sutton Manor in 1396 by Richard II. The moat was where the junction of the A4 with Sutton Court Road is today. Henry V gave orders for this house to be pulled down in 1415 but a new house must have been built shortly afterwards, since Henry VI issued state papers from Chiswick in 1441 and 1443. [1]

---

1   R Allen Brown, R Colvin & A Taylor *The History of the Kings Works*, vol 2 *The Middle Ages*, 1963, 1003

Fig 4. The village of Old Chiswick by Schnebbelie in 1807. It shows St Nicholas Church, the ferry and the riverside (Local Studies, Chiswick Library)

The Chiswick House Lake was supplied by a stream known as the Bollo or Boller Brook.[2] This rose on Hanger Hill, flowed through Acton then down Bollo Lane. Here it divided, one branch going along Acton Green, the other crossing Chiswick High Road, filling a pond on Turnham Green before going southwards down Sutton Lane and through the grounds of Chiswick House before debouching into the Thames at the end of today's Promenade Approach Road. Another stream, running west-east across Chiswick from Spring Grove, probably joined the Bollo Brook before it reached Chiswick House.[3] Today, the Bollo Brook is contained in a conduit underneath the Lake which is now supplied with water direct from the Thames.

The occupants of Old Chiswick and Strand on the Green were mainly concerned with activities connected with the river: fishing, ferrying, boat building, brewing and cultivating the osiers which grew along the water's edge (these were used for making baskets). Crops such as wheat, oats and barley were grown – the latter said to be particularly fine in Chiswick which accounts for the number of malt houses and breweries. By the middle of the 18th century, though, cereals were giving way to fruit and vegetables with market gardens and orchards replacing the fields as Chiswick and neighbouring parishes became part of the `great garden of London' to satisfy the ever-increasing demands of the Capital.

A church is thought to have been on the site of the parish church of St Nicholas since at least 1181; the tower we see at present was erected in the 15th century. Meetings of the local vestry were held in the church and a charity school was built on

2   Report of the Committee of Magistrates appointed to make enquiries respecting the public
    bridges in the County of Middlesex, 1826,191
3   Ordnance Survey Map 1865

the south side in 1707. There were almshouses for the poor at Strand on the Green, Essex Place and in Sutton Lane by the end of the 17th century and a workhouse was built in Chiswick High Road in 1725. This stood well back from the road, behind what is now Waterstone's bookshop.

Below the church is the slipway where foot passengers took the ferry across to Barnes. The ferry was no doubt busy in Lord Burlington's time since it was the only way to cross the river until Kew Bridge was built in 1759. There would have been a continual stream of traffic on the Thames itself with people going about in fishing boats, wherries, and other small craft; also grander vessels conveying owners of riverside houses to their homes, and there might also have been a glimpse of sumptuous velvets and rich brocades as Royal personages glided down the river in magnificent barges to the palaces at Kew and Richmond.

Judging by the proceedings of the Old Bailey, Chiswick was a reasonably law-abiding place – there were a few murders, many thefts and several highway robberies along the main road to the west of England (the wide expanse of Turnham Green was a favourite haunt of footpads and highwaymen). Lord Burlington was a theft victim in 1739 when one Richard Sedgewick stole a black mare. In court Sedgewick said: `I have nothing to say. I am as innocent as the child unborn, I was led into this thing very innocently'. Lord Burlington's servant John Goring said he would be happy to have Sedgewick's life spared as he was `a very weak simple fellow'. But, to no avail, he was sentenced to execution.[4]

Chiswick was caught up in the Civil War in 1642 when the Parliamentarians burnt the altar rails of St Nicholas Church and when, on 13 November, Turnham

Fig 5. An artist's impression of the Civil War battle at Turnham Green in 1642. Painting by John Hassall (Local Studies, Chiswick Library)

4   www.oldbaileyonline.org

Green, which was much larger than it is today, was the scene of a Civil War battle. Although only a skirmish, the `Battle of Turnham Green' was important since it foiled the attempt of Charles I and his Royalist army to re-take London, which was in the hands of Oliver Cromwell's Parliamentary army. The Royalists, marching towards the City, had triumphed at Brentford the previous day. Hearing of this the Earl of Essex, leader of the Parliamentarians, summoned his forces and marched to Turnham Green throughout the night. By 8am it is estimated that 24,000 Parliamentarians faced the Royalists who, being seriously outnumbered, beat a fairly hasty retreat.

In 1698 Chiswick was the scene of another threat to a monarch. A group of people, disaffected by the ousting of the Catholic King James II, hatched a plot to assassinate the new King William III on his way home from his regular hunting expedition in Richmond Park. They planned to waylay the King's coach in what is today's Wellesley Road, then a `quagmire', which was a short way from the Brentford horse ferry from Richmond. The conspirators planned to divert the King's escort and slay the monarch. However, someone who knew of the plot informed the authorities and the King put off his trip.

Burlington's Jacobean mansion

The Jacobean house inherited by Lord Burlington was arranged around four sides of a courtyard with a formal garden at the rear (see Fig 6) - `a noble seat built by Sir Edward Warden, after the ancient manner, very regular and strong. It has very many spatious rooms in it, and a large garden behind', wrote local historian John Bowack.[5] Edward Warden is almost certainly Sir Edward Wardour who erected a monument to his family in St Nicholas Church in 1612. The house is thought to date from about 1611 although excavations during 2008 revealed that it had been altered during the 17th century. The range at the rear was added and the bay windows at the front replaced by the pedimented gables shown on Fig 6.[6] Horace Walpole, who visited the house in 1760, says that it had `a good eating room in which is a monstrous heavy chimney of marble'.[7]

This house already had something of a colourful history by the time it came into the Boyle family. In 1624 it was bought by Sir Robert Carr the disgraced Earl of Somerset. Carr and his wife had been banished from court because of their involvement in the murder of Sir Thomas Overbury. Overbury was an author and intimate friend of Carr but violently opposed Carr's marriage to Frances Howard, who had divorced her first husband the 3rd Earl of Essex. The Countess arranged to have Overbury poisoned. She confessed to the murder and was imprisoned in the Tower of London for some years. After the couple were pardoned by James I they moved to Chiswick and it was here that the Carr's daughter, Anne (who had been born in the Tower) fell in love with her near neighbour, William Lord Russell (later 5th Earl and 1st Duke of Bedford) who lived in nearby Corney House. Despite opposition from the Russell family the couple were eventually allowed to marry. However, to satisfy the dowry requirements of the

5   John Bowack 'Antiquities of Middlesex', 1705/6, reproduced in WPW Phillimore & WH Whitear (eds) *Historical Collections Relating to Chiswick*, 1897, 12
6   David Fellows `Chiswick House London: Excavations on the site of the Jacobean House', *Research News the Newsletter of the English Heritage Research Department*, No. 11, Spring 2009, 7
7   Horace Walpole *Journals of Visits to Country Seats etc* Walpole Society v16, 1928

bridegroom's family, the Earl and Countess were obliged to sell all their plate, jewels and furnishings, and to mortgage Chiswick House to Philip, Earl of Pembroke. The mortgage not being paid, the Earl of Pembroke foreclosed on the property in 1638 and assigned the house to John, Lord Poulet or Pawlet, an active supporter of the Royalist cause in the English Civil War. After Poulet's death in 1649 his sons surrendered all their property in Chiswick to their mother, Elizabeth, then the wife of John Ashburnham, who had been a groom of the bedchamber to Charles I.

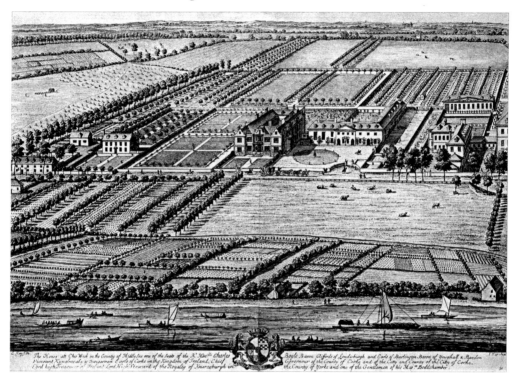

Fig 6. The Jacobean Chiswick House c.1700 by Kip and Knyff. The building to its right is the L-shaped stable block/service building. To its right are the buildings belonging to Moreton Hall with the house on the extreme right (Peter and Carolyn Hammond)

In 1664 the house at Chiswick was bought `with all that is in it' by Charles II for £7,000 for his natural son James, Duke of Monmouth. Two years later the duke gave the house to Charles, Lord Gerard of Brandon (later the Earl of Macclesfield) as part payment of the command of the Life Guards (Lord Gerard also paid £4,000). By 1676 Chiswick House was the property of the Lord Ranelagh who owned it until 1681. It was then briefly the home of Sir Edward Seymour before being acquired by Lord Ranelagh's uncle Richard Boyle, 1st Earl of Burlington.[8]

The house had a stable block and service wing (later known as the Grosvenor Wing) which was begun in the summer of 1682 by Sir Edward Seymour from whom the 1st Earl of Burlington was to buy the house in November. Accounts discovered during

---

8   Chiswick Rate books; Victoria County History Vol VII *Middlesex*; Warwick Draper Chiswick, [1923], 1973 ed,

the last ten years show that the architect of this building was Sir Thomas Fitch and not Hugh May to whom it had been credited.[9] As well as stabling and a coach house this substantial L-shaped building contained the kitchens for the house, a servants' hall, a bakery, a laundry, a washroom and a brewery.[10]

Noble neighbours

The attractions of the Chiswick riverside meant that it became increasingly popular as a country retreat for the wealthy. John Bowack, writing at about the time Burlington succeeded to the title, describes Chiswick thus:

> The pleasant village of Chiswick, tho but small, is so very pleasantly situated out of the road and free from noise, dust and hurry that it has for many years past boasted of more illustrious and noble persons than any of its neighbours.[11]

Lord Burlington did indeed have some illustrious neighbours since the Jacobean house was only one of several grand houses in the loop of the Thames between Chiswick parish church and Strand on the Green. Near the church was Corney House which had been home to the Russell family, earls of Bedford in the 17th century and, where, in 1602, they had entertained the elderly Queen Elizabeth. The house had been rebuilt at the beginning of the 18th century and between 1745 and 1754 the rates were paid by the widowed Duchess of Norfolk.

Next door to Chiswick House, surprisingly close in fact, was a very grand mansion (later known as Moreton Hall). It had been built in 1682-4 by Sir Stephen Fox, financial entrepreneur and civil servant, who became the Lord of Chiswick's Prebendal Manor. After his death in 1716 it was sold to the Countess of Northampton, mother-in-law to Fox's daughter and was inherited in 1719 by her son Spencer Compton, MP and Speaker of the House of Commons. He was created Lord Wilmington and commissioned Lord Burlington to design a new entrance hall for the house in 1732.

To the west of Chiswick House was Grove House, which had been home to the Barkers, a family of lawyers, for nearly 200 years. In 1747 Grove House was sold to the Earl of Grantham. Behind Chiswick House was Sutton Court, one of Chiswick's two manor houses. In 1704 it was lived in by the widowed Countess Fauconberg, daughter of Oliver Cromwell.

Every one of these grand properties was later to be acquired by the owners of Chiswick House and added to the Chiswick House estate – Sutton Court and its lands were leased by the 3rd Earl of Burlington in the 1720s; the 6th Duke of Devonshire purchased Moreton Hall in 1812; Corney House in 1830 and Grove House in 1833. By the middle of the 19th century the 6th Duke controlled more than half the land in the parish of Chiswick.

---

9 Richard Hewlings *The Service Buildings at Chiswick House* (unpublished paper given at the Chiswick House Conference, 2006)

10 English Heritage *Chiswick House and Grounds* nd (unpublished); David Fellows 'This Old House: Excavations at Chiswick House' *Current Archaeology*, October 2008, pp20-9

11 John Bowack see above, 1705/6

Chapter 2

THE ARCHITECT EARL
INHERITS (1704-1726)

On 9th February 1704, aged nine years and 10 months, Richard Boyle became the 4th Earl of Cork and the 3rd Earl of Burlington on the death of his father. Besides the Jacobean house in Chiswick, the property he inherited when he came of age comprised Londesborough in Yorkshire (the family home of the Boyles), Burlington House in Piccadilly and estates in Ireland. Little is known about Lord Burlington's childhood. He was educated by private tutors and lived with his widowed mother until he matured. He was described as a `good natured pretty gentleman' in 1713 when he was 19.[1]

Fig 7. Richard Boyle, 3rd Earl of Burlington and 4th Earl of Cork, oil painting by Jonathan Richardson, c.1717-19. Behind the Earl is the Bagnio, his `first architectural foray' at Chiswick (© National Portrait Gallery, London)

In 1714-15 Burlington completed his education by going on the Grand Tour. He visited the countries known today as Belgium, Holland, Germany, France and Italy. He is not thought to have shown a great interest in Classical architecture or Italian gardens during this trip, being at that time more enthusiastic about music, a love he inherited from his mother. He had been appointed Director of the Italian Opera in London when he was only 16 and he (or more probably his mother) had given the impoverished Handel rooms in Burlington House in about 1712 where Handel lived for at least two years. Burlington was the principal financial backer of the short-lived Royal Academy of Music set up under the patronage of George I in 1719.

---

1 Quoted in James Lees Milne, *Earls of Creation*, 1962, 104

While on the Grand Tour Burlington met William Kent (1685-1748), a Yorkshireman who had been sent to Rome by wealthy patrons in 1709 to study art. Burlington employed Kent to make sketches for him and perhaps as his agent to purchase pictures.

Shortly after he came of age in 1715 Burlington began remodelling Burlington House, Piccadilly (now the home of the Royal Academy). James Gibbs was the first architect employed but, by 1717, he had been replaced by Colen Campbell who was responsible for transforming Burlington House into a palatial Palladian mansion. It was at this time too that Burlington began to change the garden of his Jacobean house in Chiswick. Again, he employed James Gibbs succeeded by Colen Campbell in 1717. Burlington also commissioned from one or other of these architects (or perhaps designed himself) a small building called the Summer Parlour which was at the rear of the Jacobean house and had a China Closet on its eastern side (now a roofless ruin).

In 1719 Burlington spent three months or so visiting France and Italy. This time he visited some of the villas and gardens which were to have such a seminal influence on his own work. He also collected William Kent in Paris and housed him in rooms in Burlington House, some of which Kent decorated. Kent lived with the 3rd Earl's family for the rest of his life.

Fig 8. An owl on the moulding in Chiswick House. The owl was the symbol of Lady Burlington's family, the Saviles (© Adam Watson)

In 1721 Lord Burlington married Lady Dorothy Savile, the daughter of the 2nd Marquess of Halifax. She loved music and the stage and everything associated with it and dabbled in painting. Her letters to her husband are always affectionate and caring although she is said to have been opinionated and sharp tongued. The marriage produced three daughters, one of whom, Juliana, died aged only four. Lady Burlington survived her husband by five years.

Lord Burlington's passion was architecture and he became an able amateur architect himself, but he was also a great patron of artists, poets, writers, musicians, sculptors as well as architects. Horace Walpole describes Lord Burlington thus: `Never was protection and great wealth more generously and more judiciously diffused than by this great person, who had every quality of a genius and artist, except envy'.[2] History has given Burlington these attributes – proud, kind, compassionate, reserved, sensitive and idealistic.

---

2   Horace Walpole, *The Anecdotes of Painting in England*, 2nd ed, vol 4, 1782, 229

The amateur architect

Lord Burlington was inspired by the architecture of ancient Rome, particularly as revived by the 16th-century Italian architect Andrea Palladio and his 17th-century British disciple Inigo Jones.

Andrea Palladio (1508-1580) was a stonemason turned architect who formulated a system of architecture based on his study and measurement of ancient Roman buildings and the 10 books of Vitruvius, a Roman military architect. He considered that good architecture should be strong, useful and beautiful and that this could be achieved by symmetry and proportion. In 1570 he published his highly influential *I Quattro Libri dell'Architettura* (*The Four Books of Architecture*) which summarised his philosophy and catalogued his designs for palaces, villas and churches. Inigo Jones (1573-1652) was the first significant British architect to be influenced by Palladio's work, especially in his most important buildings, such as the Queen's House at Greenwich and the Banqueting Hall in Whitehall.

While in Italy in 1719 Burlington had purchased the English translation of Palladio's *Four Books of Architecture* and shortly afterwards bought many drawings of the designs of Palladio, Jones and John Webb (1611-1652), Jones's assistant and son-in-law). These drawings formed the basis of his substantial architectural library and were sources for his own designs.

The movement towards Palladianism in England was already beginning when, in 1712, Lord Shaftesbury, in a letter to Lord Somers, attacked the Baroque buildings of Wren and his protégés.[3] It was given further impetus by the publication in 1715 of the first volume of *Vitruvius Brittanicus* by Colen Campbell. This contained architectural drawings of English buildings inspired by Classical models, condemned the `capricious ornaments' of Baroque architecture and praised `antique simplicity' in the taste of the ancients in their gardens. It further inspired Burlington and due to his social position and political influence Palladianism became the new fashion. Palladianism dominated English architecture for the first half of the 18th century and spread through Europe and the American colonies. It has influenced building design ever since.

Lord Burlington's first architectural venture was a Bagnio (bath house) in Chiswick which he designed in 1717 (see p21), under the guidance of Colen Campbell. (As he became more architecturally mature Burlington rejected Campbell as an inferior Palladian architect.) Before he started work on the villa at Chiswick, Burlington designed several other buildings. In 1720 his brother-in-law, Lord Bruce, commissioned him to design Tottenham Park in Wiltshire (rebuilt long ago); in 1723 he designed a house for General Wade in Old Burlington Street (demolished in 1935).

After the villa in Chiswick was built, Burlington produced designs for several buildings, notably a dormitory for Westminster School in 1730 (gutted by fire during World War II), Richmond House for the 2nd Duke of Richmond, and a council building for Chichester, Sussex. In 1732 he designed a new entrance hall for his

---

3   Shaftesbury to Lord Somers `Letter Concerning the Art or Science of Design', 1712

next door neighbour Lord Wilmington at Moreton Hall and - perhaps his greatest achievement - the Assembly Rooms in York which still survive, although the façade has been remodelled. They are currently used as a restaurant. His last major design - for new Houses of Parliament in Westminster which took eight years and a hundred drawings (mostly by William Kent) was never built.

Burlington's circle

William Kent, initially a painter, branched out as an interior decorator, architect and finally a garden designer. In the process he became a fashionable architect in his own right. Some of his most notable buildings - the Royal Mews in Charing Cross (demolished), the Treasury buildings and the Horse Guards Buildings, both in Whitehall, resulted from his appointment in 1725 (through Burlington's influence) as Master Carpenter at the Office of Works. He designed furniture and interiors for Holkham Hall, Norfolk, added wings and a stable block to Rousham House, Oxfordshire and garden buildings at Badminton Park, Euston Hall and

Fig 9. William Kent by Benedetto Luti
(© Devonshire Collection, Chatsworth. Reproduced by permission of the Chatsworth Settlement Trustees)

Shotover House. He also designed for the Royal Family. For Queen Caroline (wife of George II) he designed two garden follies, known as the Hermitage and Merlin's Cave, at Richmond Lodge, and for her eldest son Prince Frederick he designed the interiors and substantially rebuilt the White House in Kew (since demolished), also a magnificent ceremonial barge which is now in the National Maritime Museum.

Kent is more famous, perhaps, as one of the pioneers of the English Landscape Movement in garden design. He did away with the rigid formal parterres, knot gardens, straight allees and topiary, common to 17th-century gardens, and let nature speak for itself `All gardening is landscape painting', he said. He designed many gardens, most notably Rousham House, Oxfordshire, Stowe House, Buckinghamshire and Claremont in Surrey.

Horace Walpole summed up Kent thus: as a painter he was `below mediocrity'; as an architect `he was the restorer of the science'; as a gardener he was `thoroughly original, and the inventor of an art which realises painting and improves nature'.[4]

It is not known how involved Kent was with the design of Chiswick House. He painted some of the ceilings, designed fireplaces and furniture for the house and

4   Horace Walpole *see above*, 235

was involved with landscaping the garden after about 1727. It is hard to believe, though, that Kent, who was after all living with the Burlington family, had no input whatsoever into the design of the Chiswick villa. But perhaps he was too busy in his new role as Master Carpenter at the Office of Works, and with his garden commissions.

Kent and Burlington were total opposites: Kent was easy going, charming, indolent and idiosyncratic, whereas Burlington was formal, austere, learned and a rigid theorist. However, their affection for each other was sincere. Lady Burlington was fond of him too; she called him `the little Signor' and took painting lessons from him. He designed a pram for little Lady Dorothy and a lady's dress ornamented with the four orders of architecture so that the lady appeared like `a walking Palladio in a petticoat'.[5]

After Kent, Burlington's most intimate friend was Alexander Pope whom he had known since he was a teenager. Pope was already an established poet in 1716 when he came to live with his parents in Mawson Row, Chiswick, and was in the throes of translating Homer's *Iliad* (some drafts of his translation were on the back of letters addressed to Mr Pope `at his house in ye New Buildings, Chiswick).'[6] His translation made Pope good money and in 1719 he moved to his villa in Twickenham where he built his famous grotto.

Pope suffered from Potts Disease (a form of TB of the spine) which stunted his growth and deformed his body. He is known for his venomous tongue and vitriolic pen, but his friendship with the Burlington household seems to have been harmonious. He teased William Kent and was sincerely attached to Lord Burlington. In a letter written in 1722, four years before Burlington built his Palladian villa, Pope wrote:

> His garden flourishes, his statues rise, his pictures arrive, and (what is far more valuable) his own good qualities daily extend themselves to all about him, whereof, I the meanest? (next to some Italian chymists, fiddlers and opera-makers) am a living instance.[7]

Pope is referring here to Italian musicians, brought back by Burlington from Italy, both to play for him and to work in the new Royal Academy of Music.

Pope and Burlington shared similar views on architecture and on gardening. In 1731 Pope wrote his *Epistle to Lord Burlington* which was later to form one of his four `Moral Essays'. Pope counsels against seeing greatness as size and dimension instead of proportion and harmony, and decrees that buildings and gardens must be adapted to the genius and use of the place:

---

5   Quoted in John Harris `William Kent' *Oxford Dictionary of National Biography*, 2004, 104
6   This house which now has a blue plaque to Pope is the building that contains the Mawson Arms pub
7   Quoted in John Harris, *The Palladian Revival: Lord Burlington his House and Gardens at Chiswick*, 1994, 48

> To build, to plant, whatever you intend,
> To rear the column, or the arch to bend,
> To swell the terrace or to sink the grot;
> In all, let nature never be forgot.[8]

Pope visited Chiswick House regularly, long after he had moved to Twickenham, often being rowed along the river, and seems to have come and gone as he pleased. In a letter written two months before his death he mentions his intention to go over to Chiswick for the day `to dine by myself before their hour', and to return in the evening because he dared not `lie abroad'.[9] In a letter he wrote to the Earl in 1742 he says `You have no Flatterer here, and I assure you, Chiswick has been to me the finest thing the glorious sun has shin'd upon'.

Lord Burlington's other regular visitors were the poet and dramatist John Gay (1685-1732), the cleric and essayist, Jonathan Swift (1667-1745), and actor and theatre manager David Garrick (1717-1779). Lord Burlington was Gay's patron and Gay lived under his roof for a while. William Thackeray described Gay as `lazy, kindly, uncommonly idle... forever eating and saying good things'. Gay wrote the following verse to Lord Burlington:

> While you, my lord, bid stately piles ascend
> Or in your Chiswick bow'rs enjoy your friends?
> When Pope unloads the boughs within his reach
> the purple vine, blue plum and blushing peach.[10]

In 1728 Gay's *Beggars Opera*, a parody of Italian opera, satirising the Court and politics of the day, was produced. Apparently Burlington never spoke to him again.[11]

Jonathan Swift, the Anglo-Irish satirist and Dean of St Patrick's Cathedral, Dublin visited Burlington on his frequent trips to England. When he visited shortly after Burlington's marriage he is said to have asked Lady Burlington to sing for him, but the peremptory manner in which he made his request apparently reduced her to tears. In 1726 Pope helped Swift to arrange the anonymous publication of the book now known as *Gulliver's Travels* which became an instant and enduring success.

A later visitor to Chiswick was David Garrick, the most distinguished actor of his day and theatre manager of Drury Lane. In 1749 Garrick married Eva Marie Veigel, a Viennese dancer known as `La Violette' and described by Horace Walpole as the `finest and most admired dancer in the world'. Lady Burlington invited her to stay at Burlington House and part of the honeymoon was spent at Chiswick.

Was La Violette Lord Burlington's love-child? A rumour to this effect was published in *Notes and Queries*.[12] Apparently Lord Burlington, passing the dancer's room in

---

8   Alexander Pope *Epistle to Richard Boyle, Lord Burlington*, 1731
9   Quoted in Jessie McGregor *Celebrated Gardens and Gardens of Celebrities*, 1918, 178
10 John Gay *Epistle to the Right Honourable Earl of Burlington, a Journey to Exeter* 1715
11 Jenny Uglow *Hogarth*, 1997, 136
12 *Notes and Queries* 25th January 1873

Burlington House, had noticed a miniature of La Violette's mother and identified her as a lady who had left his protection for that of another, telling him that their daughter had died (this, in case Lord Burlington should attempt to claim her). The source of the rumour is said to have been the housekeeper at Burlington House at the time Lord Burlington made the discovery. Whether it is true or not, Lord Burlington gave La Violette £6,000 on her marriage to Garrick.

Possibly less harmonious was Burlington's relationship with the artist William Hogarth who became his near neighbour in 1749. Hogarth was a quintessentially English painter who wanted to improve the status of English artists. As such he was out of step with the artistic preferences of the time which harked back to the Classical themes promoted by the art patrons of the day, notably Lord Burlington. He called them `imitators and mannerists' and lampooned them in his prints.

In the background of Hogarth's *Masquerades and Operas* (1724) is the Palladian gateway to Lord Burlington's Piccadilly mansion. On top of the pedestal, with the supporting statues of Michelangelo and Raphael bowing in reverence, William Kent wields his palate and waves his paintbrush giving aristocratic sanction to the taste of the London crowd. It is captioned `ACADEMY OF ARTS' – a citadel of false taste.

Another salvo against the Burlington-Kent clique was fired in 1741 in a print entitled *The Burlington Gate* and attributed to Hogarth. It shows Alexander Pope and Lord Burlington attempting to whitewash the `gate of good taste' with William Kent directing their work. In the process whitewash is being splattered on Lord Chandos who was patron of James Thornhill, Hogarth's father-in-law.

William Kent was Hogarth's particular bête noire `never was there a more wretched dauber', said Hogarth. His dislike of Kent was no doubt further fuelled by the fact that Kent received the commission to paint the new rooms of Kensington Palace instead of Thornhill who was Sargeant Painter to the King. Perhaps there is some significance in the fact that Hogarth only bought his `little country box' in Chiswick, just to the north east of Chiswick House, the year after William Kent died. Hogarth himself died in 1765 and is buried in a fine tomb in St Nicholas Churchyard, Chiswick with an inscription composed by David Garrick. He is, though, just a few feet away from his old enemy Kent who is buried in a vault beneath the chancel!

However, Hogarth did accept commissions from the Burlington family (Hogarth was not averse to accepting favours from those of whom he disapproved). He is thought to have painted the figures in his friend George Lambert's views of Chiswick House.

Work on the gardens

There are few records or accounts of work on the Chiswick House gardens; most of what is known or surmised about the dates for the various features comes from illustrations, and Chiswick House has the distinction of being visually recorded more than any other 18th-century garden. Lord Burlington first commissioned the Flemish artist Pieter Andreas Rysbrack to produce eight oil paintings probably between 1728 and 1732. In 1733 he commissioned the French topographical painter Jacques Rigaud to paint eight watercolours. However, they fell out after Burlington felt that Rigaud was trying to overcharge him. In 1736 John Rocque produced his engraved survey of Chiswick with boxed drawings showing the individual buildings (see Fig 1). George Lambert was asked for two oil paintings in 1742. Finally, in the 1750s, John Donowell produced six engravings of the garden. As well as the commissioned pictures, William Kent produced many sketches of designs for the garden and a few whimsical drawings of both house and grounds.

Fig 10. The Patte d'oie by John Donowell in the 1750s. The Bagno is the building at the end of the left hand avenue; the Domed Building terminates the central avenue; the Rustic House, the right hand avenue (Local Studies, Chiswick Library)

The illustrations, though, cannot be relied on to depict the gardens accurately. One of Rysbrack's oils shows a second deer house which was probably never built. Rigaud and Rocque both show a stone bridge across the Lake, for which there is no evidence (the bridge was made of wood), and both show designs for an Orangery which differ from the Orangery finally erected. Rocque also shows a Cascade when none had been started and a plan of Lady Burlington's Flower Garden with an aviary which excavations in 2008 failed to discover. And the balustraded platform on top of the Cascade shown in one of George Lambert's pictures seems to have been pure artistic licence.

The young Lord Burlington began changing the garden belonging to the Jacobean mansion ten years before he built his Palladian villa. There doesn't appear to have been any overall plan, the Chiswick garden was designed on a very ad hoc basis. First Burlington laid out the three avenues known as the Patte d'oie (French for goose's foot) because of its resemblance to the webbed foot of a goose. Each avenue terminated in a small building.

The building at the end of the left hand avenue was known as the Bagnio (bathhouse) or Casina and was the Earl's initial architectural foray at Chiswick in 1717. The architect Colen Campbell, Burlington's architectural mentor, described the Bagnio as 'the first essay of his Lordship's happy invention'. Burlington used the building as his drawing office and placed the statues of Inigo Jones and Andrea Palladio outside. These are long thought to have been sculpted by Michael Rysbrack (brother of Pieter Rysbrack, the painter). However, it has been suggested that they were actually the work of Giovanni Battista Guelfi whom Burlington had brought back with him from Italy in 1715, since Guelfi sculpted busts of both Palladio and Jones which are strikingly similar to these statues.[13] Once the Villa was built the statues were moved to stand outside it.

At the end of the central avenue was the Domed Building, sometimes called the Pavilion or Pagan Building. It is thought to have been the work of James Gibbs in 1716. The right hand avenue was terminated by the Rustic House, probably designed by Lord Burlington in about 1720. Just off the avenue leading to the Rustic House was a bowling green, surrounded by sweet chestnut trees.

A visitor standing at the head of the Patte d'oie could in fact see six radiating avenues, each with a focal point. The avenue on the far left led to a statue depicting Samson slaying the Philistine (sometimes called Cain and Abel and thought to have been sculpted by Guelfi), then avenues terminating in the Bagnio, Domed Building and Rustic House, followed by an avenue leading to a Doric Column, built before 1728, and topped with a statue of the Venus de Medici, and finally an avenue to a Deer House, probably of Lord Burlington's own design in about 1720.

Fig 11. View of the Doric Column with the Venus de Medici statue by William Kent (© Devonshire Collection, Chatsworth. Reproduced by permission of the Chatsworth Settlement Trustees)

This served a small enclosure for deer which Burlington created in the area between the Jacobean house and its near neighbour Moreton Hall (see p53), and was separated from the garden by a ha-ha (sunken fence).[14] The function of the deer house is not properly known although deer houses were quite a common feature of houses of this period. It was perhaps

---

13 Richard Hewlings 'The Statues of Inigo Jones and Andrea Palladio at Chiswick House', *English Heritage Historical Review*, vol 2, 2007, 76

14 Ha-Has are thought to have been introduced to England by garden designer Charles Bridgeman so as to provide an uninterrupted view of a park. As it suggests, the term is thought to have been an exclamation of surprise. Horace Walpole says they were 'deemed so astonishing that the common people called them ha-has! to express their surprise at finding such an unperceived check to their walk'. (*Anecdotes of Painting in England*, 2nd ed, vol 4 1782, 288)

Fig 12. View of the Temple by the Water, with the basin, the long canal and the new wooden bridge by Pieter Andreas Rysbrack, c.1730 (© Devonshire Collection, Chatsworth. Reproduced by permission of the Chatsworth Settlement Trustees)

where the deer were given the supplementary food they need when their antlers are growing, or maybe it was just intended to be an ornamental garden building. There was another entrance to the deer park where the Inigo Jones Gateway is today.

The Bollo Brook on the other side of the garden was initially the boundary of Lord Burlington's grounds. Here, two oblong basins of water parallel to the Brook were created, both with semi-circular ends, one framed by topiary, the other beside a building known as the Temple by the Water (probably designed by Lord Burlington) and described by a visitor in 1779 as 'a very neat building that represents the portico of St Paul's Church, Covent Garden'.[15] Horace Walpole, who visited in 1760, says this building contained 'some Massive seats with beasts for arms, designed by Inigo'.[16]

Squeezed between these water basins was the Orange Tree Garden, shaped as an amphitheatre, surrounding a circular pool with an obelisk in its centre and a circular temple with an Ionic portico. This must have been in position by 1726-7 as it was given an additional entrance after the garden was extended over the water. Orange trees in tubs had been placed on the tiers of the amphitheatre by 1729.The lawn at the back of the house was covered in a dense plantation of trees, known as the Grove, probably planted in 1715.[17]

15 *The Modern Universal British Traveller*, 1779, 380

16 Horace Walpole *Journals of Visits to Country Seats*, Walpole Society vol 16, 1928, 22

17 The type of trees is not known; it is thought they may have been poplars or elms

This is how the garden is thought to have appeared prior to Lord Burlington acquiring land on the other side of the water in 1726-7, and before the involvement of William Kent. More changes and additions were made after 1733 when Lord Burlington made Chiswick his official London home.

Fig 13. The Orange Tree Garden, Obelisk and Ionic Temple by Pieter Andreas Rysbrack, c.1730
(© Devonshire Collection, Chatsworth. Reproduced by permission of the Chatsworth Settlement Trustees)

Chapter 3

THE NEW VILLA (1726-1758)

In 1721 Lord Burlington had given his Jacobean mansion a new Palladian façade but in 1725 the house caught fire and the west wing was destroyed and demolished. Lord Burlingon didn't restore it but built a one-storey extension to replace it. The fire was perhaps the spur Burlington needed to design a new free standing villa. This was built 18 metres west of the old house and further back from the road.

He mined his extensive library of architectural drawings for design ideas for each individual feature of his villa. It is often said that Chiswick House is modelled on Palladio's Villa Capra (La Rotonda) at Vicenza. Burlington did indeed borrow ideas from the Rotonda and from others of the 30 or so country villas built by Palladio, but he also borrowed from Scamozzi's Villas Molini and Rocca Pisani, from the designs of Inigo Jones and from the buildings of ancient Rome itself. He moulded all these elements into what is a unique and individual neo-Classical composition.[1] Burlington began to build his villa in 1726. He used his bricklayer from Burlington House, Richard Wright, and when Wright died Burlington buried him in Chiswick churchyard in a splendid tomb thought to have been designed by William Kent.

Many of the drawings for the Villa were made by Henry Flitcroft (1697-1769). Flitcroft came to Burlington's notice after falling from a scaffold and breaking his leg while working as a carpenter during the reconstruction of Burlington House. Lord Burlington paid for his convalescence and, noting his talent for drawing, employed him as his draughtsman and assistant between 1720 and 1726. As a result of Burlington's patronage Flitcroft was appointed as Clerk of the Office of Works (the government building agency) in 1726. He later became a major Palladian architect in his own right, designing amongst other buildings, Woburn Abbey, Wentworth Woodhouse and many of the garden temples for Henry Hoare's Stourhead.

It took a year to dig out the foundations for the Villa at Chiswick. Built in brick and faced with Portland stone, it was completed in 1729.

The architects Burlington used at Chiswick were all involved with the large Palladian villas that exist today. The earliest, Mereworth Castle, Kent, was designed by Colen Campbell between 1720 and 1725. Campbell also designed Stourhead, Wiltshire for banker Henry Hoare with Henry Flitcroft responsible for some of the eyecatchers in its garden. James Gibbs, Colen Campbell and William Kent were all involved

---

1 For details of the buildings etc that influenced Burlington's designs see `Chiswick House and Gardens: Appearance and Meaning' by Richard Hewlings in *Lord Burlington Architecture, Art and Life*, edited by Toby Barnard and Jane Clark, 1995; *The Palladian Revival: Lord Burlington, His Villa and Garden at Chiswick* by John Harris 1994.

Fig 14. View of the new villa, old house and stables from across Burlington Lane, by Pieter Andreas Rysbrack c.1729 (© Devonshire Collection, Chatsworth. Reproduced by permission of the Chatsworth Settlement Trustees)

with Houghton Hall, Norfolk and Colen Campbell, William Kent and probably Lord Burlington himself with Holkham Hall, Norfolk.

How the house is arranged

Burlington's villa is a 70ft square two-storey building with a dome (modelled on the Pantheon in Rome) with an outside double staircase front and back. The steps at the front lead to a portico with pillars of the Corinthian order. The present obelisk-shaped chimneys are 1950s reconstructions of the original obelisk chimneys which don't seem to have been very efficient (probably due to insufficient up-draught) and had been replaced by conventional chimneys by the time Rocque carried out his survey in 1736 (see Fig 1).

Inside the house, both floors have a central octagonal hallway surrounded by rooms of different geometric shapes – circular, square, rectangular and octagonal. This combination of room shapes was novel at the time the house was built. Today visitors enter on the ground floor with its rather stark Tuscan-style interior. It is not known how these rooms were used in Lord Burlington's time apart from the fact that he had his library (after 1733) on the garden side in three interconnecting rooms – one circular, one rectangular with apses and the third an octagon. The library bookcases, designed by William Kent, are now at Chatsworth, Derbyshire (home to the Dukes of Devonshire).

The central hall was probably used as a waiting room for people wanting to see the Earl, and there was a wine cellar off the gallery. When an inventory was taken in 1770 (17 years after Burlington's death) two of the downstairs rooms were furnished as bedrooms and two others were a butler's pantry and a linen room.

Fig 15. Andrea Palladio's Villa Capra in Vicenza, Italy. Photographed in 1977 (© Adam Watson)

Unlike the ground floor, the upper storey is rich in decoration and ornamentation with painted ceilings and lashings of gilded mouldings. The octagonal hall (known as the Tribunal or Saloon) is carried up to the roof level under the dome. The Gallery above Lord Burlington's library leads to the sumptuous Blue Velvet Room and Red Velvet Room on one side; the Green Velvet Room and Bedchamber on the other. Lady Burlington died in the Bedchamber surrounded by tapestries based on an original Teniers design. Later, Charles James Fox was to die in the same room (see p50).

The two floors are connected inside only by three narrow spiral staircases which would have been difficult for ladies in full skirts to negotiate. Visitors in Lord Burlington's time would have entered by the outside staircase to the first floor.

The house was filled with good furniture, many pieces designed by William Kent, but very little of the house's original furniture remains today; it was removed sometime in the late 19th century when the Dukes of Devonshire leased out Chiswick House. Some went to Chatsworth; other pieces were sold but are being bought back when they appear on the market. Still to be seen, though, are five embroidered chairs in the Green Velvet Room. These were part of a set of gilded furniture supplied to Lady Burlington for her Garden Room (see p33). The two large porphyry vases in the Gallery were brought back from Italy by Lord Burlington. Also in the Gallery are four mahogany hall chairs (part of a set of 16) designed by Kent for the house, and a pair of side tables with inlaid marble tops and gilded wooden bases. These, also designed by Kent, somehow found their way to the Scottish home of the Marquess of Bute, a tenant of Chiswick House (see p75), and were purchased in 1996. When Chatsworth turned out its attics in 2010 and sold the contents by auction, seven lots relating to Chiswick were acquired by English Heritage and are now back in the House.

Most of Lord Burlington's fine collection of paintings has also gone. The best of these were in the Green Velvet and Red Velvet rooms. The Tribunal or Saloon originally contained sculpture and the eight large paintings hanging there today probably came to Chiswick House in 1733 when Lord Burlington transferred them from Burlington House. The 1770 Inventory records more than 137 paintings, including works by Rembrandt, van Dyck, Velasquez, Poussin, Veronese and Kneller. There was also, according to Horace Walpole, who visited in 1760, `a bad picture of Lady Euston and Lady Hartington, the Earl's daughters, by Kent'! [2]

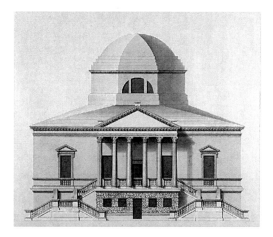

Fig 16. Elevation of the front of Chiswick House by Henry Flitcroft (© Devonshire Collection, Chatsworth. Reproduced by permission of the Chatsworth Settlement Trustees)

Why did he build it?

Lord Burlington left no record of his reason for building the villa so we can only guess at his intentions. It certainly wasn't built as a house to live in, since it had no kitchens or servants' quarters, or proper internal stairs. and the upstairs rooms are a peculiar, and hardly cosy, arrangement for bedrooms, each linking to the adjoining room. It might also have been rather cold since not every room had a fireplace.

Neither does the theory that the house was built for extravagant entertaining hold much water since there is no correspondence (or none that has survived) from people who went to parties at Burlington's Chiswick villa.

With the wing of the old house demolished Burlington probably needed a new gallery in which to display the paintings and sculptures he had acquired on his travels. The villa may have been just an architectural experiment, an attempt to create a Classical masterpiece. A theory advanced in the last decade by Jane Clark and others is that Lord Burlington built Chiswick House as a Masonic temple.

Burlington may have been a freemason, like his friends William Kent and Alexander Pope. Many educated and successful men became masons in the early 18th century after the founding of the first Grand Lodge in 1717. It is argued that Lord Burlington was an important Masonic figure since he features in verse six of a song quoted in *The Constitutions of the Free-Masons* by Dr James Anderson in 1723:

2   Horace Walpole *Journals of Visits to Country Seats*, Walpole Society vol.16, 1928, 22

Then in our songs be justice done,
    To those who have enrich'd the Art,
From Jabal down to Burlington
    And let each Brother bear a part
Let noble Masons' Health's go round
    Their praise in lofty Lodge resound [3]

Freemasonry was also the preserve of the Jacobites (supporters of the restoration of the Stuart kings to the throne). Lord Burlington, although a grandee member of the Whig party, is also thought to have been a closet Jacobite. He apparently appears on the list of people willing to support the restoration of the Stuarts to the throne in the event of a successful invasion. These lists were sent to James in Rome in 1733 and 1743. Burlington is said to have provided money for the cause and this is advanced as a reason why his finances became so depleted. The thistles, roses, bunches of grapes and pomegranates carved into the fireplaces in the Red Velvet Room and the oak leaves and Prince of Wales feathers elsewhere are said to be Jacobite badges.

Fig 17. Box garden plan of Chiswick House laid out in the gardens of Chatsworth
(© Devonshire Collection, Chatsworth. Reproduced by permission of the Chatsworth Settlement Trustees.)

Those who support the Masonic theory point out that the colours of the rooms in Chiswick House – green velvet, blue velvet, red velvet – do not conform to conventional 18th-century interior decoration schemes (although they are of course good colours to use as backdrops for works of art) and could represent different degrees of masonry – blue, the colour of the craft masons, red the colour of the 'Royal arch' masons and green often associated with the higher degrees of masonry. The

---

3   Quoted in Jane Clark 'Lord Burlington is Here' Toby Barnard & Jane Clark (eds) *Lord Burlington, Art, Architecture and Life*, 1995, 297

Fig 18. Ceiling of the Blue Velvet Room painted by William Kent and entitled An Allegory of Architecture (© Adam Watson)

dimensions of the rooms, number of steps and chimneys are also claimed by some to be elements of Masonic ritual.

It is suggested too that Masonic symbols are encrypted in the painted ceilings. The ceiling in the Blue Velvet Room, painted by William Kent, for instance, is entitled *An Allegory of Architecture* and shows putti holding compasses/dividers, plumb lines and set squares. These are all symbols of freemasonry, deriving as masonry is thought to do, from the medieval guilds of skilled stone masons who travelled around Europe building the great cathedrals. But then perhaps architectural implements are understandable in a painting for an eminent amateur architect.

Some of the garden structures can also be construed as having Masonic meanings – the Ionic Temple (representing the Temple of Solomon), obelisks (the sun and astronomical phenomena), and the sphinxes (riddles, arcane myths and the occult).[4] Whether the Masonic theory is true or not, one cannot help feeling there is something in the suggestion by John Cornforth writing in *Country Life*: `the villa gives me the uncomfortable feeling that it contains elements which uninitiated people are not supposed to understand'.[5]

4   For information on the Masonic elements of Chiswick House, see Jane Clark `Lord Burlington
     is Here' (see above) and Ricky Pound `Chiswick House – a Masonic Temple?' *Brentford &
     Chiswick Local History Journal*, vol 16, 2007, 4

5   John Cornforth, `Chiswick House, London' *Country Life*, 16th February, 1995, 32

What people thought about Chiswick House

The architecture of Chiswick House would have seemed quite novel to Burlington's contemporaries. Apart from Inigo Jones, and his son-in-law John Webb, a century earlier, English architects were not building in the neo-Palladian style. Today, everyone is familiar with neo-Palladian or neo-Classical architecture since, due to the influence of Lord Burlington and his followers, it is the style used for many public buildings such as the White House in Washington and Buckingham Palace.

Reactions to Burlington's new building were mixed. William Aikman who saw it under construction wrote to his cousin Sir John Clerk of Penicuik `His [Lord Burlington's] house at Cheeswick is near finished and is a very beauty'[6]. Sir John was less impressed when he himself visited in 1727, calling it `rather curious than convenient'.[7]

Fig 19. Gilded Corinthian capitals in Chiswick House (© Adam. Watson)

A distinguished party of visitors in 1732 reported that `both within and without, it is a fine bijou'.[8] Local historian Daniel Lysons in 1761: `his Lordship has erected a beautiful villa which, for elegance of taste, surpasses everything of its kind in England'[9] and Thomas Boydell in 1794 that it would grace the banks of the Arno or the Tiber.[10]

Kielmansegge, a German visitor in 1761 was less complimentary: `It must be admitted that the house is built in the best taste but it is much too small, and gives the impression of being a model of a house of larger dimensions'.[11] The size of Burlington's villa was the subject of the famous gibe by the waspish Lord Hervey: `A house? Do you call it a house? Why it is too little to live in and two large to hang on one's watch chain'.[12] George II's son Prince William Augustus, Duke of Cumberland dismissed it as `a small cupboard stuck with pictures.' There was a more considered verdict from Horace Walpole: `a model of taste, though not without faults, some of which are occasioned by too strict an adherence to rules and symmetry '.[13]

6   Quoted in Cinza Maria Sicca `Lord Burlington: Architecture and Landscape', *Garden History*, Spring 1982, 54

7   Quoted in John Harris *The Palladian Revival* see above, 107

8   Quoted in Jessie McGregor *Gardens of Celebrities and Celebrated Gardens in and Around London*, 1918, 163

9   Daniel Lysons *London and its Environs*, 1761, 112

10 Thomas Boydell *History of the River Thames*, 1794-6

11 Count Frederick Kielmansegge *Diary of a Journey to England in the Year 1761-2*, 1902, 157

12 Quoted in John Harris *see above*, 107

13 Horace Walpole *Anecdotes of Painting in England*, 2nd ed, vol 14, 1782, 232

The writer Walter Scott, who visited in 1828, wrote that `the place and highly ornamented garden belonging to it, resembles a picture by Watteau.'[14] But not everyone admired Burlington's garden: `the grand walk, which forms the first point of view, being planted with cypress-trees, intermixed with urns and funeral monuments in the antique taste, has the appearance of a burying ground: it seems to form an avenue leading to the temple of melancholy', wrote Jean Pierre Grossley in 1772.[15] The great Thomas Jefferson, later President of the United States and the designer of his own Palladian house, Monticello in Virginia, gave both Chiswick House and its garden the thumbs down when he visited in 1786. He opined that the house's octagonal dome `has an ill effect, both within and without' and that `the garden still shows too much of art...an obelisk of very ill effect; another in the middle of a pool - useless'.[16]

Lord Burlington set a fashion when he admitted visitors by ticket to view his house and pictures, but only when the family was in residence. However, William Watts who visited in 1779 (after Burlington's death) met with `very disagreeable treatment' when he was found making sketches of the various buildings.[17]

Changes to the garden

In 1726 and 1727 Lord Burlington was able to extend his garden by purchase and lease of three parcels of land on the far side of the Bollo Brook, one parcel being the southern area of the land belonging to the Sutton Court manor house. It was about this time too that William Kent is thought to have become involved with the garden, designing new garden buildings and landscaping the formal garden features into softer shapes.

Fig 20. View of the garden through one of the Venetian windows (© Adam Watson)

The move away from formal gardens to a more naturalistic layout had begun at the beginning of the 18th century. Joseph Addison writing in the *Spectator* in 1712 suggested that parks and rural scenery could be successfully integrated. Alexander Pope satirized the excessive artificiality of topiary in an article in the *Guardian* in 1713: `There was Adam and Eve in yew; Adam a little shatter'd by the fall of the Tree of Knowledge in the great storm...'. Batty Langley wrote in his introduction to the *New Principles of Gardening* in 1728 `Nor is there anything more shocking than a stiff regular garden'. Charles Bridgeman was an early pioneer of the more naturalistic garden and it is he who is credited with

---

14 Walter Scott diary entry 17/5/1828
15 Jean Pierre Grosley *A Tour to London or New Observations of England and its Inhabitants*, vol 2, 1772, 117
16 Thomas Jefferson *Jefferson's Garden Book*, 1854, 10
17 William Watts *The Seats of the Nobility and Gentry*, 1779

introducing the ha-ha, or sunken fence to open up vistas and keep livestock from encroaching onto the lawns. However, it was William Kent who saw that `all nature is a garden' and working `without line or level' imposed a new irregularity in garden design, paving the way for Lancelot (Capability) Brown's landscaped gardens later in the century.

Fig 21. Classical sculpture on the Obelisk by the Burlington Lane Gate
(Chiswick House and Gardens Trust)

Once he had acquired the new land, Burlington moved his deer to a larger park on the other side of the water. The former small deer park possibly became a pheasantry before a later Orangery (see p37) was built there. Now that the Bagnio (see p21) and Ionic Temple (see p22) were accessible from both sides, it was necessary to give them second entrances. The Bagnio was enlarged and the Ionic Temple given a rear porch.

The new land was laid out as a wilderness garden with straight avenues leading to the Bagnio and the Ionic Temple and winding paths leading elsewhere. Visitors to Chiswick House were now able to enter through a new gateway in Burlington Lane and drive up to the house over the Lake through a water splash. In front of the new Burlington Lane gate an Obelisk was erected in 1732 and an antique sculpture placed on its base. This bas relief had been rescued from a pile of building rubble by the Earl of Burlington and once formed part of a large collection of Classical statuary assembled by the Earl of Arundel in the 17th century.[18]

Besides the two entrances from Burlington Lane there was another carriage entrance to Chiswick House through the large arch, next to the Rustic House (see p22). The compiler of the third edition of Daniel Defoe's *Tour Thro the Whole Island of Britain* mentions a `coach road through the gardens by which his Lordship passes when he comes to London so that the Earl seldom goes thro' the town of Chiswick to his home'.[19]

The Bollo Brook had been widened by Burlington into a straight canal. This was now remodelled into a serpentine river and the soil excavated from this (and probably also from the water basins) was used to form the Raised Terrace. This was planted with `all manner of sweet shrubs, roses, honeysuckle etc.'[20] and provided views over

---

18 *Gentleman's Magazine*, July 1769, 352
19 Daniel Defoe *A Tour 'thro the Whole Island of Great Britain*, 3rd edition 1742, 290
20 Daniel Defoe *A Tour 'thro the Whole Island of Great Britain*, 2nd edition 1738, 202

the meadows across the Thames. It was possible to see the Pagoda in Kew Gardens after it was built in 1762.

Trees on the western side of the Grove which abutted the villa were cleared away and a semi circular enclosure with iron railings created by c.1728. In about the same year it is thought that what might have been a maze was laid out on the lawn leading to the river.

In front of the house, eight Cedars of Lebanon[21] were planted in the forecourt which was also lined with terms (stone plinths ending in a sculpted human face).[22]

Lord Burlington moves to Chiswick

In 1733 Lord Burlington made Chiswick his main London residence. There is much speculation as to why he took this step. It might have been pique at not being offered a court appointment promised by the king, but given instead to the Duke of Devonshire, or the fact that Burlington went into opposition over the Whig Party's introduction of the Excise Bill, a customs tax on wine and tobacco. Whatever the reason, Burlington wrote to George II resigning all his court appointments, packed up the best of his pictures from Burlington House and retreated to Chiswick.

The Jacobean house and the Palladian villa were connected by the small structure known as the Link Building and a Loggia (a two-storey covered area attached to the Link Building and the Jacobean house). It has long been thought that these were not erected until Lord Burlington's move from Piccadilly to Chiswick. However, the discovery in the 1990s of accounts kept by Henry Simpson, whom the Duke appointed as his agent for all his estates in Great Britain in 1725, suggests this work was begun prior to 1733. These accounts show that payment for a major construction, which can only be these buildings, was made in 1732. This suggests that the complex was fully complete before Lord Burlington made Chiswick his London home.[23] Some question whether this was really such a drastic a move since Lady Burlington did not resign as Lady of the Bedchamber to Queen Caroline until two years later and the Burlingtons continued to use the house in Piccadilly.

At Chiswick, William Kent fitted out the Summer Parlour (see p14) as Lady Burlington's Garden Room with an accompanying flower garden. Kent designed the furniture which Lady Burlington apparently paid for out of her own pocket. A sketch by Kent shows Lady Burlington relaxing in her flower garden attended by her black servant James Cambridge. The sketch also shows an aviary which is also present on John Rocque's 1736 plan where it is described as a *volerie*. Whether it was built or not is uncertain since excavations in 2008 revealed no trace of it.

---

21 Since the cedars seem quite mature in the illustrations by Rysbrack and Rigaud it is possible they were transplanted from Sutton Court.

22 Term is short for *termini* or terminal figure. Terms are sometimes referred to as Herms although these usually carry the bust of Hermes.

23 R T Spence `Chiswick House and Gardens 1726-1732', *The Burlington Magazine* vol 135, August 1993, 525

Fig 22. Design for Lady Burlington's Flower Garden with James Cambridge, Lady Burlington's black servant (© Devonshire Collection, Chatsworth. Reproduced by permission of the Chatsworth Settlement Trustees)

William Kent now progressed with landscaping the garden. More trees were cleared from the Grove, the maze (if that is what it was) was grubbed up, allowing a large expanse of lawn to sweep down to the Lake (this was a revolutionary bit of garden design at the time). Urns, cypress and cedar trees lined the avenue through the centre of the garden; two stone sphinxes had been added by 1742, another, lead sphinx, carved by John Cheere was placed there in 1749. This was one of three lead sphinxes commissioned from Cheere; the other two were placed on the gate piers in the Forecourt. They were removed to the gates at the Duke's Avenue entrance by the 6th Duke of Devonshire and are now in Green Park (see p56). Sphinxes are considered guardians of a property (or, in Masonic terms, symbols to ward off the uninitiated).

Kent designed a semi-circular termination at the end of the lawn, known as the Exedra. Work on it began in 1733. Kent's drawings show that he originally intended the backdrop to be a stone screen but, instead, a dark yew hedge was planted, which provided a better contrast to Lord Burlington's collection of statuary and was less expensive.

The statues in the Exedra were installed a year or so later. They included a lion and lioness, probably designed by Peter Scheemakers, and three antique statues which are said (probably incorrectly) to represent Caesar, Pompey and Cicero and were brought back from Rome by Lord Burlington. They apparently came from the Villa Adriana at Tivoli, east of Rome. This was built by Roman Emperor Hadrian in the early 2nd century. `Villa' seems a bit of a misnomer for this massive complex which covered over 250 acres. It fell into disuse with the decline of the Roman Empire but began to be excavated in the 16th century and excavations continue today. During the 18th century many of its statues were sold to people on the Grand Tour.

Large urns were installed in the Exedra, also more terms (these with male heads, those in the forecourt have female heads). In addition, there were 12 senatorial stone benches, said to come from the Forum at Rome but now thought to be English-made. Other statues in the gardens included a copy in Portland stone of the famous Calydonian Boar statue in the Uffizi Gallery, Florence. Burlington's statue was probably carved by Peter Scheemakers, as was its companion, a wolf (both are now at Chatsworth). These two statues stood at the back of the house, looking towards the Exedra.

There was also a lead figure of Mercury supplied by James Vermynck in 1729; a goat (sculpted by Michael Rysbrack), a lead gladiator, and a lead representation of Hercules at either end of the Arcade around the Orangery, a marble statue of Apollo Belvedere in an elevated niche, busts of the Roman emperors Trajan and Vitellus set into recesses in the outside wall of the Summer Parlour.

In 1737 the Lake was changed again, its edges softened and landscaped to give a better illusion of a river. The following year the Inigo Jones Gate came to Chiswick.

Fig 23. William Kent's first design for the Exedra
(© Devonshire Collection, Chatsworth. Reproduced by permission of the Chatsworth Settlement Trustees)

Fig 24. The Orangery, detail from John Donowell's view of the back front of the house and part of the garden (© Adam Watson)

This had been designed by Inigo Jones in 1621 for Beaufort House in Chelsea. It was acquired by Lord Burlington when his friend Hans Sloane was in the process of demolishing Beaufort House. It replaced the pedimented door to the Deer Park which was transferred to what is now the entrance to the Hockey Field. The flanking walls to the Inigo Jones gate were probably put up in 1738. This poem, written about the gate, is long thought to have been penned by Alexander Pope but is now thought to be by William Kent:

> Ho! Gate, how came ye here
>   I came from Chelsea last yere,
> Inigo Jones there put me together;
>   There was I dropping by wind and weather
> Sir Hannes Sloane let me alone;
>   But Burlington brought me hither.[24]

Burlington decided to install an artificial cascade alongside the watersplash on the entrance from the Burlington Lane Gate. The Cascade was problematic from the outset. A number of sketches by William Kent survive which show that various

---

24 Quoted in John Harris *see above*, 253

designs were considered before the present rocky structure with three arches was decided upon. But it was still unfinished in 1738 and it never worked properly. A visitor in 1742 [25] said that it had failed hydraulically and engineers were still being asked to fix it in 1748. The engine house to power the Cascade might have been inside the tall octagonal tower shown on a print of 1750 engraved by Fougeron.

Burlington's next – and last – structure for the Chiswick House garden was a new Orangery in what had formerly been his small deer park. This might be because a winter shelter was needed for the citrus trees displayed in the Orange Tree Garden. Again, there were various different designs, some by William Kent, and others by Burlington himself. The final design was a rectangle consisting of five arches, an entablature and balustrade and divided by Corinthian columns. The building has now gone but its mosaic floor remains under a covered platform. Archaeologists excavating it in 2009 think the floor is contemporary with the building.

Lord Burlington's latter years

Lord Burlington's last architectural drawing is dated 1735, after which `Burlington Architectus', as he signed his drawings, ceased to practice. His final years do not appear to have been too happy. His mounting debts meant that no new work was carried out at Chiswick and there were family problems.

In 1741 his elder daughter Lady Dorothy, known as Dolly, married Lord Euston, the great grandson of Charles II and Barbara Villiers,[26] and son and heir to the Duke of Grafton. Within seven months Dolly was dead. She had contracted smallpox but her death is said to have been

Fig 25. The Burlington Lane Gate and the Obelisk in the moonlight with Kent sitting by the Obelisk with rabbits at play
(© Devonshire Collection, Chatsworth. Reproduced by permission of the Chatsworth Settlement Trustees)

hastened by her husband's ill treatment. Lord Burlington challenged Euston to a duel; Euston accepted the challenge but the duel was prevented.

---

25 Daniel Defoe, 3rd edition 1742 *see above*

26 Barbara Villiers, Lady Castelmaine, lived in Walpole House, Chiswick Mall for the last two years of her life (1707-9) and is buried in Chiswick Parish Church

Lady Burlington painted a picture of Dolly which still hangs in Chiswick House. On it is the inscription:

> Lady Dorothy Boyle, born May the 14th, 1724. She was the Comfort and Joy of her Parents. The Delight of all who knew her Angelic Temper, and the Admiration of all who saw her Beauty. She was marry'd October ye 10th, 1741, and Deliver'd (by Death) from misery, May 2nd, 1742. (This picture was drawn seven weeks after her Death (from Memory) by her most affectionate Mother). Dorothy Burlington.'

In 1745 Burlington's younger daughter Lady Charlotte Boyle became engaged to Lord Hartington, heir to the Duke of Devonshire, and married him in 1748. The Burlingtons were delighted to have a son-in-law who was `a young nobleman with the best character and the greatest hopes'.[27] The engagement, however, caused such a terrible rift within the Devonshire family that the Duchess left her husband, so strong were her feelings against the match. The reasons are not known but it is suggested by Jane Clark [28] that Burlington's Jacobite sympathies were suspected by the Devonshires. The 4th Duke was a prominent Whig statesman, appointed First Lord of the Treasury which meant he was the titular Prime Minister of Britain.

In 1748 Burlington's great friend William Kent died, leaving his money to his mistress the actress Elizabeth Butler and their two children. There seems to have been some rift between `Kentino' and Lord Burlington in the latter years, the cause of which is not known, but Kent's last letter to Burlington from Paris is very penitent: `…but for yr confidence I have in yr goodnesse for my pardon. I know you are not ignorant of yr cause wch induc'd me to it, from a most unworthy proceeding…' [29] However, Burlington buried him in the Burlington Vault under St Nicholas Church in Chiswick.

Lord Burlington himself was ailing; he suffered from the palsy. By 1751 his signature had become shaky and a special `machine chair' was ordered. He died at Chiswick in 1753 aged 59 and was buried at Londesborough. He left his whole estate in trust to his widow with the instructions that on her death the estate should pass to his daughter Lady Charlotte, Baroness Clifford,[30] but Charlotte predeceased her mother, dying in 1754 aged only 23. Chiswick, along with Burlington's other properties, passed, on Lady Burlington's death in 1758, to William Lord Cavendish, the eldest of Charlotte's four children and future 5th Duke of Devonshire.[31]

Opposite: Fig 26. Plan of the Chiswick House estate in 1753 (© Ken Reilly)

---

27 Quoted in Jane Clark `Lord Burlington is here' see above, 285
28 *Ibid*, 284
29 Quoted in James Lees Milne *The Earls of Creation*, 1962, 130
30 Will of the Earl of Burlington; Public Record Office The National Archives; cat ref: Prob 11/812
31 Will of Dorothy, Countess of Burlington; Public Record Office The National Archives; cat ref: Prob 11/1840

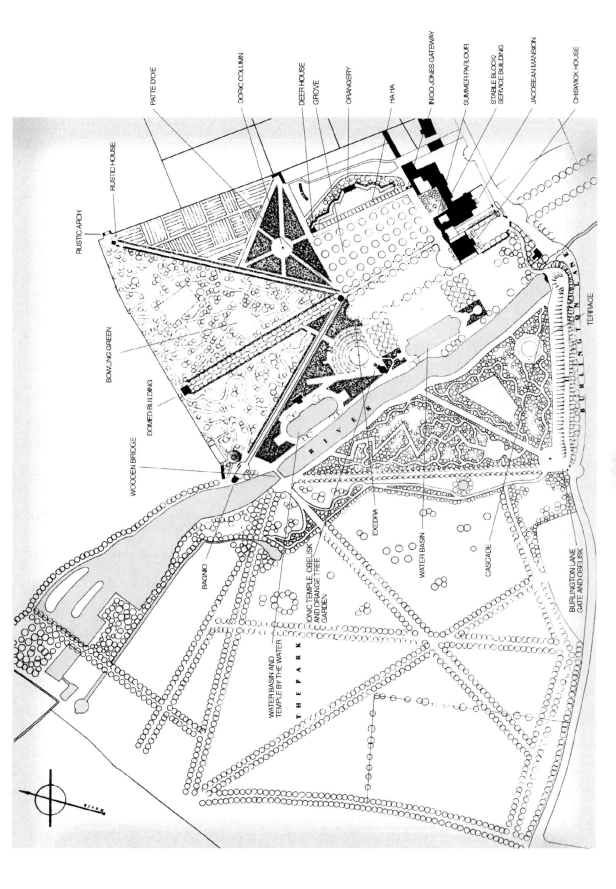

RUSTIC ARCH

RUSTIC HOUSE

PATTE D'OIE

DORIC COLUMN

DEER HOUSE

GROVE

ORANGERY

HA-HA

INIGO JONES GATEWAY

SUMMER PARLOUR

STABLE BLOCK/
SERVICE BUILDING

JACOBEAN MANSION

CHISWICK HOUSE

BOWLING GREEN

DOMED BUILDING

WOODEN BRIDGE

BAGNIO

WATER BASIN AND
TEMPLE BY THE WATER

IONIC TEMPLE, OBELISK
AND ORANGE TREE
GARDEN

THE PARK

EXEDRA

WATER BASIN

CASCADE

BURLINGTON LANE
GATE AND OBELISK

BURLINGTON LANE

TERRACE

RIVER

NORTH

39

Chapter 4

'MY EARTHLY PARADISE' (1758-1811)

William Cavendish (1748-1811) succeeded his father as the 5th Duke of Devonshire in 1764. In 1774 he married Lady Georgiana Spencer on her 17th birthday. Sadly, it was something of a mismatch. The Duke, although clever, seems to have been a lethargic, taciturn, unemotional sort of fellow, roused only by card games and devoted to his dogs. Georgiana on the other hand was a lady of magnetic charm, loving and beloved by all who met her. She became the queen of society and the fashion icon of her day. She was intelligent and creative, composing music, poetry and publishing (anonymously) a novel called *The Sylph*. The Prince of Wales, playwright Richard Brinsley Sheridan and politician Charles James Fox were among her intimate friends.

Fig 27. William Cavendish, the 5th Duke of Devonshire by Pompeo Girolamo Batoni

But she was a creature of paradoxes; she was an inveterate gambler running up gambling debts which haunted her throughout her life, and she had a lover, Charles Grey (Prime Minister between 1830 and 1834, and the man who gave his name to Earl Grey tea) with whom she had an illegitimate daughter, Eliza Courtney (this caused her husband to banish her to France for two years).

Georgiana became an active and astute supporter of the Whig party. She organised entertainments to raise party morale, many of them held at Chiswick, but she is perhaps more celebrated as one of the first women to canvass votes on behalf of a political party. Her interest in politics had been kindled by meeting Charles James Fox in 1777. In 1784 Fox was standing for the constituency of Westminster in the General Election, where there were three candidates, but only two seats. Voting at the hustings, set up in Covent Garden, took six weeks. Devonshire House served as the headquarters for Fox's campaign with great feasts taking place there every night. Georgiana, her sister and other grand Whig ladies, took to the streets to persuade people to vote for Fox. They hobnobbed with tradesmen, bought trinkets from them in exchange for promises of votes, and offered them lifts to the hustings in their grand carriages. Georgiana is also said to have exchanged kisses for votes. This was thought scandalous and Georgiana became the subject of many satirical cartoons. However, the efforts of Georgiana and her cohorts were successful and Fox won his seat, although the Whig party lost the election overall. A triumphal procession of carriages and horses made its way back to Devonshire House with Fox carried in a chair.

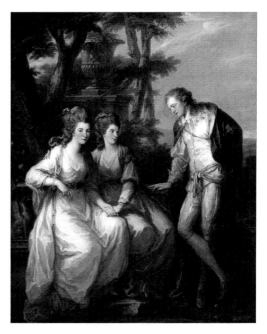

Fig 28. Georgiana with her sister and brother, picture entitled Lady Georgiana, Lady Henrietta and George John, later 2nd Earl Spencer by Angelica Kauffman
(from the Collection at Althorp)

Devonshire House was also the centre for intrigue and jockeying for position within the Whig Party during the `Regency Crisis' of 1788 caused by the illness of George III. Medical opinion was divided as to whether his disorder was mental or physical (it is now thought it was the blood disease porphyria). If the Prince of Wales was installed as Regent, the government would have to resign, and the Whig party saw this as an opportunity to gain power as the Prince of Wales was their friend and supporter. The crisis was averted when George III regained his health in early 1789.

The Prince of Wales and Georgiana were close friends – they referred to each other as `brother' and `sister' (Georgiana tapped him – among others - for money to pay her gambling debts). He greatly admired Georgiana, sought her advice on many matters, and at the ball to mark his official presentation to society in 1781, displeased the ladies of the court by dancing with Georgiana all night long.

However, Georgiana found it distasteful when the Prince involved her in his romantic affairs. He had fallen for Maria Fitzherbert, a respectable widow who refused to become his mistress and whom he was forbidden to marry because she was a Roman Catholic. In 1784 he claimed to have attempted suicide and declared his dying wish was to see Mrs Fitzherbert. She refused to go to him unless Georgiana accompanied her. When the ladies arrived at Carlton House they found the Prince spread on a sofa draped in bandages. He begged Mrs Fitzherbert to marry him and she reluctantly agreed, the pact sealed by a ring borrowed from Georgiana. After the `engagement' both ladies took the precaution of signing a note stating that `promises obtain'd in such a manner are entirely void'.[1]

---

1   Quoted in Earl of Bessborough (ed) *Extracts from the Correspondence of Georgiana, Duchess of Devonshire*, 1955 ,87

The following day they found out they had been duped – the Prince's suicide had been faked to trap Mrs Fitzherbert. She promptly went abroad and Georgiana wrote a stern rebuke to her `brother' telling him not to come to Chatsworth unless asked. But the Prince did `marry' Mrs Fitzherbert eighteen months later. Georgiana was invited to be one of the witnesses. She wrote to the Prince saying the whole thing was madness, and: `I cannot be present for it is not a marriage. & I cannot be by at what I do not think one.' [2]

For 25 years the Duke and Duchess lived in a curious ménage à trois with Lady Elizabeth Foster, known as Bess. Separated from her husband and two sons she was fairly destitute and gave the impression of being rather frail. She was pretty, witty and intelligent and boasted many admirers, notably the historian Edward Gibbon. She met the Devonshires in Bath in 1782 and was welcomed into their household where she lived on and off until both the Duke and Duchess were dead. She was, however, rather affected and many people considered her something of an adventuress, particularly Lady Spencer, Georgiana's mother, who resented the leech-like hold Bess had on her daughter. Georgiana was extremely fond of Bess referring to her as `my dearest, dearest, dearest angelic love'. The Duke was fond of her too – perhaps too fond: she bore him two illegitimate children. But the friendship between the three of them was real and enduring. They gave each other nicknames. The Duke was `Canis' because of his fondness for dogs, Georgiana was `the Rat' for reasons which are not known and Bess was `Racky' perhaps because of her constant racking cough. Bess supported Georgiana through her illegitimate pregnancy and kept vigil by Georgiana's bedside during her dying days. After Georgiana's death Bess paid her this

Fig 29. Cartoon showing Georgiana kissing a butcher for his vote during the 1784 election
(© Trustees of the British Museum)

tribute in a letter to her son: `She was the only female friend I ever had…our hearts were united in closest bonds of confidence and love…she doubled every joy, lessened every grief. Her society had an attraction I never met with in any other being.'[3]

The Devonshire marriage produced three children: Georgiana in 1784, nicknamed `Little G'; Henrietta (Harriet) `Haryo' in 1785, and finally in 1790, a son and heir,

---

2   *Ibid*, 88
3   Quoted in Amanda Foreman *Georgiana, Duchess of Devonshire*, 1999, 373

William Spencer George, Lord Hartington known as `Hart'. But they were not the only children in the Devonshire household. Besides Little G, Haryo and Hart, there were the two children produced by the Duke and Bess – Augustus Clifford and Caroline St Jules - and later Bess's two sons by her ex-husband. There was Charlotte Williams, the Duke's illegitimate daughter by his mistress Charlotte Spencer, born in 1774, and adopted by the Devonshires on the death of her mother, also a young French girl, Corisande de Grammont. She was the granddaughter of Georgiana's friend the Duchesse de Polignac and daughter of the Duc de Grammont. Georgiana offered to look after her when her mother contracted tuberculosis. For much of the time too, there was Caroline Ponsonby, the daughter of Georgiana's sister Harriet. Caroline later married William Lamb and is famous as the Lady Caroline Lamb who had a tempestuous affair with Lord Byron.

Fig 30. 'Bess', Lady Elizabeth Foster by Sir Joshua Reynolds (© Devonshire Collection, Chatsworth. Reproduced by permission of the Chatsworth Settlement Trustees)

This coterie of kids was presided over by their governess, Selina Trimmer. Selina was the daughter of the philanthropist and author, Sarah Trimmer, one of the pioneers of the Sunday School Movement. The Trimmers lived in Brentford, the next village to Chiswick. Selina took up her duties in 1778. She stayed with the family until the children were grown up and remained a friend and confidante to Haryo.

At Chiswick

Georgiana loved Chiswick more than any of her other homes. She referred to it as `sweet chiz' and her `earthly paradise' and formed an ambitious plan to restore it in accordance with Lord Burlington's original drawings. She planted lilac, honeysuckle and climbing roses outside her window so that her bedroom would smell sweet throughout the spring and summer.

Haryo complained that the days at Chiswick `had not one inch of difference' and that her father was wont to snore `in happy forgetfulness of us all'.[4] But, after the formality of Devonshire House and the grandeur of Chatsworth, Chiswick was a haven offering Georgiana and her family a peace they craved. Haryo writes to her sister in August 1804: `We are very comfortable here. I sit out of doors the whole

4   Quoted in Sir George Leveson Gower & Iris Palmer (eds) *Hary-O The Letters of Lady Harriet Cavendish 1796-1809*, 1948, 304

morning, reading…and in the evening we go on the water by moonlight and walk till supper'.[5]

Georgiana's favourite spot in the gardens was apparently the Orange Tree Garden. It was during the tenure of the 5th Duke that the plinth outside the Orange Tree Garden was put up. It is a tomb to a favourite dog with a Latin inscription which reads in translation:

Fig 31. Lilly's Tomb', monument with a Latin inscription to a favourite dog. It stands just outside the Orange Tree Garden (© Adam Watson)

Beneath this monument lies Lilly, a little dog and the most good-natured of all dogs, of long time a most beloved companion, and in beauty and loyalty, a model of canine genius. She was free of the weaknesses of humankind while manifestly exhibiting its virtues. She was entirely without malice, but not without love. This tomb, and her mistress's tears bear witness to her virtues. Her memory will not perish from the earth.

An entry in account books in the Chatsworth Archive [6] suggests that the monument had been erected by 1804 *(June 1st £28 paid to Mr Wood for a pedestal erected in the garden to the memory of Lillie by His Grace's order)*.

So who owned the dog? The 5th Duke's favourite dog was certainly called Lilly and he took his daughter down to Chiswick for the express purpose of inspecting Lilly's puppies. Haryo wrote to her sister:

He really thinks of little else and the whole time of dinner and supper he feeds and watches them, laughs excessively every time they squeak or run and listens to no conversation with half the pleasure as he does when the puppies are the subject. [7]

However, this diary entry is for November 1807 so this could not be the dog commemorated on the monument. The inscription anyway says that the dog's owner was female which suggests that it belonged to either Georgiana or Bess.

---

5   *Ibid*, 97

6   J Fletcher's Account Book p.139; Chatsworth Archives

7   Quoted in Sir George Leveson Gower & Iris Palmer (eds) *Hary-O The Letters of Lady Harriet Cavendish 1796-1809*, 1948, 304

Bess did own a dog called Lill. It is recorded in her diary entry of May 25th 1788, when she was in Rouen awaiting the birth of her second illegitimate child by the Duke She writes:

> The apartment tolerable, but in a close confined street on one part and a stinking court on the other –The Physician comes to me sometimes, but else poor Lucille [her maid] and Lill [her dog] are my only resources. [8]

Bess's dog Lill would have been quite ancient in 1804 - over 16 years old. But, given the fact that the Devonshire family, along with many of the nobility, were often extremely slow in paying their bills, the dog might have died some years earlier and the monument constructed long before 1804. And then again Lilly might have been a name frequently used by dog owners in the Devonshire family

One of the first changes to the Chiswick estate made by the 5th Duke was to replace the wooden bridge over the `Chiz' river by the stone Classic Bridge in 1774. It is said to have been designed by Jeffery Wyatt but a more likely candidate is James Paine, famous as a bridge designer, who was also on a retainer to the 5th Duke. Avray Tipping writing in *Country Life* says of the bridge `a better example – fine in line and rich in detail – does not exist in England of the Classic treatment of this kind of structure'.[9]

Fig 32. The Classic Bridge, erected in 1774 to replace a wooden bridge (© Adam Watson)

The Jacobean Chiswick House was now old and probably run down and when the children came along the Devonshires needed more nursery space. So, the 5th Duke had the house demolished and, in 1788, added two wings to Burlington's villa to transform it into a proper country mansion. The wings are thought to have been designed by James White, a little known architect who was Surveyor to the Duke of Portland (a friend of the 5th Duke). Wyatt, who was still on a retainer to the Duke, might also have had a hand in the design. The wings were Palladian in style, of graceful proportions and not as high as the dome. But they were monumental compared to the small and delicate villa. The house and wings were connected by a lower lobby and a long curved corridor was built to join the east wing to the service building / stable block which still apparently retained the kitchens and service quarters. [10] Tastes in gardening had changed and in 1784/5 the 5th Duke employed Capability Brown's assistant, Samuel Lapidge, to de-formalise the garden. In reply to Lapidge's description of the intended alterations the Duke wrote: `you mention in your last letter

---

8   Quoted in Dorothy Margaret Stuart *Dearest Bess* 1955

9   H Avray Tipping `Chiswick House, Middlesex I' *Country Life*, Feb 9th, 1918, 137

10   English Heritage *Chiswick House and Grounds* nd (unpublished)

Fig 33. Chiswick House from the garden showing the wings added by the 5th Duke of Devonshire. Picture by J Gendall, 1823 (Chiswick House and Gardens Trust)

that the expence proposed might be lessen'd which I should be glad to have done, as I don't reside much at Chiswick'. [11]

However, quite a lot of work did take place. The straight avenues of the Patte d'oie (see p20) were planted over, the Bagnio (see p21) and Domed Building (see p21) demolished in 1778 and 1784 respectively. The avenue leading to the Bagnio was realigned on the Classic Bridge. The Temple by the Water (see p22) and the water basins were also removed some time after 1784.

The curving Serpentine Walk and other paths were made by the 5th Duke and William Murfin, the Duke's gardener, spent a lot of time in 1792 creating a `Ladies Garden'. Its whereabouts is not known. It might have been a revamp of Lady Burlington's flower garden, or perhaps it was the Rosary around the Doric Column which is first recorded by a visitor in 1811 as having `120 varieties of roses'. Charles James Fox and Georgiana were great admirers of Napoleon and it was probably due to them that the large bust of Napoleon by the Danish sculptor Thorwaldsen was installed in the Rustic House (it is now inside Chiswick House). The path to the Rustic House became known as Napoleon's Walk.

---

11 Quoted in *Chiswick House Grounds Historical Survey*, Travers Morgan Planning for the Department of the Environment, 1983

The Duke's alterations to the garden did not always meet with the approval of his wife. In a letter to her mother dated 23rd December 1798 Georgiana wrote:

> Chiswick is very comfy, but, alass, the Duke and Laperidge [sic] together have play'd the deuce in the garden, they have entirely cut down the trees of the new walk he made last year. It looks like a new shrubbery. However, son' muta, I see he does not like it to be criticised and it will look better by and by, but the genius of Chiswick is gone from that part. [12]

It is apparent too that the Palladian Villa was beginning to deteriorate.

In 1793 Georgiana's mother wrote to her daughter `I am grieved at the accounts I hear of the dry rot at Chiswick',[13] and, in January 1809 Haryo tells Hart: `the rains poured with such violence into my old room the other night that I was obliged to remove to yours.'[14]

The Devonshire family lived a very peripatetic life, endlessly moving from one grand house to another, or travelling abroad. They did, however, manage to spend quite a lot of time at Chiswick, especially during the Duke's latter years. Letters written from Chiswick suggest that in some years he stayed for quite long periods. In 1805 Bess records in her journal that the Prince of Wales had lent his special carriage to take the Duchess to Chiswick. In November of the same year Haryo writes to her sister: `We are settled here for ever. Papa, I'm sorry to say has the gout and has determined to be confined here'. [15] It was also at Chiswick in 1805 that Georgiana received the news of the Battle of Trafalgar and the death of Nelson and had to inform Bess who was reading Herodotus in the Gallery with her daughter Caroline. Bess had recently met Nelson and become an ardent admirer.

Fig 34. Cartoon showing the Duchess falling into the arms of Charles James Fox as the Duke accosts them about the 1784 election expenses
(© Trustees of the British Museum)

In 1809 the family was based in Chiswick from January to March: `it snows, it rains, `tis cold, `tis dim', writes Haryo to Hart on January 29th. And on the 31st she tells her brother about her maid being attacked by one of the American deer with the result that `we are all afraid of

---

12 Quoted in *The Earl of Bessborough* see above, 230
13 *Ibid*, 200
14 George Leveson Gower & Iris Palmer (eds), *see above*, 293
15 *Ibid*, 130

going too far from the house and F Foster [Bess's son] walks with his sword drawn'.[16] The Duke and Bess were back in Chiswick in August and stayed there until April 1810.

Chiswick was obviously a place of retreat in times of trouble. The first part of the Devonshire's honeymoon was spent with Georgiana's parents in Wimbledon but a

few days later the Duke - who didn't like the regime of early rising and sensible meals at his mother-in-law's house - took Georgiana to Chiswick, and he retreated there straight after Georgiana's death. Georgiana escaped to Chiswick in 1780 to avoid the Gordon Riots, a Protestant uprising against repeal of a bill for more Catholic emancipation. This bill was supported by the Whig party, with the result that the mob, whipped up by Lord George Gordon, began to attack the mansions of Whig grandees.

In 1796, after a terrible eye infection and a subsequent operation which robbed her of the sight in one eye, Georgiana went to Chiswick to recover. When she was there again in July 1797 she says in a letter to her mother apologising for not writing earlier:

Fig 35. The Duchess of Devonshire holding a tall staff, the yellow signpost of which says `to Chiswick' (© Trustees of the British Museum)

…tho I was up…as early as anyone at church [presumably St Nicholas], but I had so much to do about the house and the gardens and the dairy. Oh, how I wish you were here, I think you would like it and `tho there is nothing but simple arrangements and quiet employments yet I never saw my dear children in better looks or wilder spirits'.[17]

Georgiana's knowledge about Chiswick's transport links was obviously a little lacking as in May 1795, when she was due to dine with her sister and brother-in-law, Lord and Lady Bessborough, in Roehampton, she took the wrong ferry and ended up in Barn Elms, rather than Kew where the Bessborough coach was waiting for her: `I had to walk near three miles in the heat and dust', she grumbles.[18] Presumably she took the ferry from just by St Nicholas Church which went to Barnes, instead of the ferry by Kew Bridge which went to Kew.

---

16 *Ibid*, 293
17 The Earl of Bessborough, *see above*, 225
18 *Ibid*, 214

Chiswick was also a favourite place for entertaining: Georgiana wrote to her mother from Devonshire House in June 1802: 'On Saturday I am to have my great breakfast at Chiswick… as the Duke allowed me to choose I own I preferred Chiswick to any assembly here, which would have been very hot & fatiguing and more limited as to numbers.' [19]

The London Chronicle in 1783 reported on a 'most elegant breakfast' given by the Duke and Duchess of Devonshire at Burlington House, Chiswick, attended by the Prince of Wales and a select number of the nobility:

> The natural beauties of this delightful spot were enlivened on this occasion by the most pleasing decorations…the trees and shrubberies were hung with festoons of flowers, displayed in easy and unaffected variations. All the figures [statues] were ornamented with sashes of roses, intermingled with oranges and myrtles.

The party began at 1pm, tea, coffee, chocolate, fruit and ices were served and the guests left at 4pm.

It was at Chiswick too in 1800 that Georgiana held one of her most lavish entertainments. Lady Jerningham, a guest describes it thus:

> We accordingly found her [Georgiana] sitting with Mrs Fitzherbert by an urn. Several Bands of Musick were very well placed in the garden, so that as soon as you were out of hearing of one Band you began to catch the notes of another; thus harmony always met your ears…there is a Temple which was destin'd to be the Prince's Entertainment and was very prettily decorated with flowers…there were about 20 covers and when we understood that the Duchess and these Fine People were in the Temple, we Goths took possession of the House where we found in every room a table spread with cold meats, fruit, ice and all sorts of wine. It is a fine House and there are the most delightful pictures in it. [20]

Lady Jerningham was presumably not close enough to hear the conversation between the Duchess and Mrs Fitzherbert. It would probably have been rather strained since Mrs Fitzherbert had never forgiven Georgiana for trying to prevent her 'marriage' to the Prince. This marriage had in fact been declared illegal under English law and the Prince had gone on to marry his cousin Princess Caroline of Brunswick. But, by the date of Georgiana's entertainment, the Prince and Princess had separated and Mrs Fitzherbert was again living with the Prince.

Departures

In 1806 Georgiana fell ill with what at first was thought to be jaundice but was in fact an abscess on her liver. She died at Devonshire House on 30 March 1806 and was buried in the family vault at Derby. She was only 48 years old. On hearing of her

---

19 *Ibid,* 248
20 Quoted in Amanda Foreman, *see above,* 334

death the Prince of Wales remarked sadly: `the best natured and best bred woman in England is gone'.[21]

Her death was followed in the same year by the death of her friend, Charles James Fox at Chiswick. Fox, then the Foreign Secretary, developed dropsy in August 1806 and his condition quickly deteriorated. The Duke offered him Chiswick House as a quiet refuge from London. There, on 13 September, he died in the room called The Bedchamber, just off the Green Velvet Room. He died just yards away from Moreton Hall, the house next door (see p12), which had been home to his grandfather Sir Stephen Fox.

Georgiana's death meant that Bess's situation in the Devonshire household was now rather precarious. This seems to have been anticipated by Georgiana who had safeguarded her friend's position to some extent by appointing Bess guardian of her letters and papers. However, the Devonshire children and the world in general considered her position anomalous. And Bess didn't help herself by acting in a proprietorial manner, accepting and giving invitations, and doing the honours as female head of the household, which rightly should have been the role of the unmarried Harriet. This must have been particularly irksome for Haryo who had never liked Bess, as she told her brother in October 1809:

> My mind was early opened to Lady Elizabeth's character, unparalleled I do believe for want of principle and delicacy and more perverted than deceitful, for I really believe she hardly herself knows the difference between right and wrong. [22]

But one must have some sympathy for Bess. She had after all lived for over 20 years as part of the Devonshire ménage and she and the Duke were in some ways akin to an old married couple.

Rumours began to circulate that Bess and the Duke were to marry. Sheridan said that she had confided to him that she thought it her `severe duty to become Duchess of Devonshire' (Bess denied this).[23] The Duke's children were dismayed. The normally placid Little G, now Lady Morpeth, described the engagement to Hart as `this painful event'.[24] Three years after Georgiana's death, however, the Duke did marry Bess. The wedding seems to have been something of a bungled affair, judging by the report in *The Universal Magazine*:

> MARRIED At Burlington House, Chiswick, the Duke of Devonshire and Lady Elizabeth Forster [*sic*]. The ceremony was performed by the Rev Mr Priddy, Chaplain to His Grace, in the presence of only two gentlemen of the Doctors Commons. Owing to a blunder committed by a person who was sent express, in a post chaise and four, for certain necessary documents, the marriage ceremony was delayed until midnight. The

---

21 *Ibid*, 390
22 George Leveson Gower & Iris Palmer (eds) *see above*, 329
23 Quoted in Dorothy Margaret Stuart *see above*, 149
24 Quoted in Amanda Foreman *see above*, 395

intentions of the parties were kept so secret that no branch of the house of Cavendish was prepared for the event.[25]

It was not until four days later that the Duke notified his son – and then only because the event had appeared in the press. Hart sent him a curt reply and wrote to his cousin:

> Hardly till I see it can I believe that woman could have the assurance to take that name always sacred to us, and henceforward to be so polluted. I don't see how I am ever going to speak to her again with patience.[26]

Georgiana's sister Harriet, however continued her friendship with the Duke and his new Duchess. She attended a house party at Chiswick in May 1810 which she describes thus:

> We have had such a posse at Chiswick! Nothing could be gayer or more brilliant, and some of the people pleasant. Each day, we sat down 26 or 27 to table, waltzing every night and all night long. 22 guests are all "inhabitants", which seems wonderful, but all are lodg'd.[27]

The Duke died suddenly in 1811, aged 62, and Hart had a problem removing Bess from Chiswick. She had assumed the Duke would allow her to keep Chiswick as a dower house and insisted that he had written a codicil to his will which gave her Chiswick for life. When it was explained to her that there was no codicil, she retorted that it must have been mislaid or destroyed and became difficult. She was given a week to pack her bags and leave the house. Hart, though, increased her allowance and gave her money to buy furniture and fittings for a new home. `Thank God I have got rid of the Duchess at last',[28] he wrote to his grandmother. Bess built a small house in Richmond but after five years moved to Rome where she spent the rest of her life.

Hart and his widowed stepmother did become reconciled. He corresponded with her and visited her in Rome. When she became ill in 1824 Hart went to Rome and was at her bedside when she died. He brought her back to England to lie in state at Devonshire House and then buried her in Derby alongside her dear friends, Canis and the Rat.

---

25 *Universal Magazine* vol XII, November 1809
26 Quoted in Amanda Foreman *see above,* 396
27 H Avray Tipping `Chiswick House, Middlesex II' *Country Life* February 16th, 1918, 163
28 Quoted in Dorothy Margaret Stuart *see above,* 183

Chapter 5

THE BUSY BACHELOR DUKE (1811-1858)

Hart was only 21 when he came into his substantial inheritance. There were the two London houses – Burlington House and Devonshire House, both in Piccadilly – as well as Chiswick House, Chatsworth, Hardwick Hall, Bolton Abbey, Londesborough, Lismore Castle, plus land in Ireland and in eight English counties. Chatsworth, luxurious and vast, was the Duke's main residence. He provided it with a new wing, designed by Jeffrey Wyatt who became Sir Jeffrey Wyattville. According to Lord Granville the celebrations on its completion were immense: 40 people sat down to dinner every day and were attended by 150 servants. `There was about Chatsworth', the neighbouring Duke of Rutland grudgingly admitted, `a splendour and magnificence to which I never did or could aspire'.[1]

The Duke appears to have been an amiable man, adored by his sisters, and very hospitable. He was an enthusiastic collector, mainly of books, sculptures, pictures, coins and medals. He was also keen on architecture and gardening. But he was extravagant, with little sense of financial responsibility, and spent so lavishly on his properties, his travel and his collections that before too long expenditure exceeded income (the Cavendish finances had not been helped of course by the high living of his parents).

The Duke moved in court circles. He represented George IV at the coronation of the Emperor Nicholas I of Russia in 1826 and held the traditional Devonshire office of Lord Chamberlain to the King under George IV (who invited him to his birthday dinner in 1827) and William IV. The Duke's letters suggest, though, that he was a trifle lonely. He was partially deaf which is often advanced as the reason he did not play an active role in politics, but perhaps he just was not that way inclined, and he never married. He had a long-term mistress, Elizabeth Warwick and in 1828 installed her in a house he owned close to Chatsworth. An entry in his diary at the end of 1828 records: `Unalloyed happiness with Elizabeth'.

The Duke's closest friends were apparently his gardener, Joseph Paxton, and his architect Sir Jeffrey Wyattville. He was also friendly with Charles Dickens, whom he invited to Chatsworth, and with George Canning, appointed Prime Minister in April 1827. Canning became ill and was invited by the Duke to recover at Chiswick. Sadly he died there, aged 57, after just 119 days in office. He expired in one of the wings to the house just after 4am on the morning of 8th August. According to Augustus

---

1   Quoted in John Pearson *Stags and Serpents*, 1983, 127

Granville Stapleton, a crowd, which subsequently amounted to between three and four thousand people, congregated outside the lodge at Chiswick.[2]

In 1837 the Duke embraced religion and his place of worship was a revivalist chapel in Turnham Green, Chiswick, meetings being held in a schoolroom above the chapel. A letter from a rather shocked Joseph Paxton to his wife back in Derbyshire tells her that the Duke was quite happy to `sit at a school bench – among the rag-tag and bobtail of the place'.[3] Later that year Paxton wrote: `the Duke is becoming a ranting, canting saint'. The Duke's new found Christian faith meant the end of his ten-year relationship with Elizabeth Warwick. She was discarded, but with generous financial provision.

Expanding the Chiswick estate

In 1812 Moreton Hall (see p12), the mansion next door to Chiswick House, came up for auction following the death of its last owner, the waspish diarist, Lady Mary Coke. It was a very grand house described by Daniel Defoe in 1725 as `the flower of all the private gentlemen's palaces in England'.[4] When William III visited in 1691 he is reputed to have paid what for him was a great compliment: `This place is perfectly fine. I could live here for five days'.[5] But when architect Samuel Ware surveyed the estate for the 6th Duke, prior to the auction, he described it as `out of repair and in a style of building not suited to the common opinion of superior beauty of modern architecture'.[6]

Fig 36. `Hart', William Spencer George Cavendish, 6th Duke of Devonshire by George Hayter (© Devonshire Collection, Chatsworth Reproduced by permission of the Chatsworth Settlement Trustees)

The 1812 sales particulars illustrate how magnificent Stephen Fox's house had once been: the `capital dining room, 35ft long by 27ft broad' had richly gilded doors, and a fireplace with carvings by Grinling Gibbons; the withdrawing room was `enlived with costly tapestry, executed to a design by Teniers'. There was a private chapel, wainscoted with oak and panelled

2 Quoted in Elizabeth Balch `Glimpses of Old English Houses: Chiswick House' *English Illustrated Magazine* 1888/9, 98
3 Quoted in John Pearson *see above*, 135
4 Daniel Defoe *A Tour 'thro the whole Island of Britain*, 1725, II, 19
5 *Ibid*, 19
6 Moreton Hall, Chiswick. Report and Valuation by Mr Samuel Ware (Chatsworth Archive L/52/12).

Fig 37. Detail from William Hogarth's only known picture of Chiswick, showing Moreton Hall, in the 1740's the home of the Earl of Northumberland. The 6th Duke of Devonshire purchased the estate in 1812 (Peter & Carolyn Hammond)

with marble and a basement with `accommodation of every description placed beneath massive and groined arches'. In the 18 acres of grounds there were `Pleasure Gardens, Paddocks, Flower-Garden, Conservatory, extensive Walled Kitchen Garden, Melon Ground, Hot-house, Stable-Yard, Double Coach-House, Stabling for Fourteen Horses' and various outbuildings including a piggery and an ice house.[7]

All that remains of Sir Stephen Fox's estate can be seen from the back of the Chiswick House Conservatory [8] - a pair of wrought iron gates set between fine red brick piers with stone cappings, balls and bases, in an old brick wall. These led into Sir Stephen Fox's walled garden, now the Chiswick House Southern Walled garden.

The Duke purchased the Moreton Hall estate for £7,050 and promptly demolished the house, incorporating its grounds into the gardens of Chiswick House. He then embarked on a mammoth scheme of changes to his new land. In 1812 *The Morning Chronicle* reported that 150 men had been employed upon the grounds for the last six months.[9]

On the same axis as the old house, but to its north, he commissioned Samuel Ware, to build a conservatory, 302ft long and 16ft wide which was completed in 1813. At the time it was one of the largest glass houses in the country and thus a forerunner of

---

7   Sales Particulars for Moreton Hall 1812 (Chiswick Local Studies Collection)
8   Sir Stephen Fox's own conservatory remained until sometime before 1865
9   *Morning Chronicle* 19th November, 1812

Decimus Burton's glass house at Kew and Joseph Paxton's Crystal Palace (Ware went on to design the Burlington Arcade, Piccadilly which opened in 1819).

Behind the Conservatory, and running its whole length, brick sheds were built for storage and to house the six coal-fired furnaces which heated the Conservatory by hot air via an underfloor hypocaust system. Irrigation was from large stone cisterns placed above the furnaces with pipes taking water to taps in the Conservatory.

On the steps in front of the Conservatory two Coade Stone (an artifical stone) vases were placed; one a copy of the antique Medici vase (now in the Uffizi Gallery, Florence); the other a copy of the Athenian Borghese vase (Louvre Museum, Paris).[10]

The Duke also asked a young garden designer called Lewis Kennedy to lay out a semi-circular `Italian' garden in front of the conservatory. Kennedy produced ideas for laying out the whole of the new grounds as a volume of watercolour drawings called *Notitiae*. Kennedy's design for Chiswick was influenced by the Empress Josephine's rose garden at Malmaison. His family firm Kennedy & Lee, one of the largest nurseries in the London area, had supplied plants to the Empress and Kennedy himself had worked for her. His design seems to have been carried out with the exception of a balustrade to separate the conservatory from the flower garden and various water features.

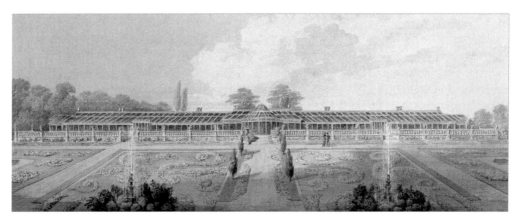

Fig 38. Lewis Kennedy's design for the Italian Garden, taken from Notitiae
(© Devonshire Collection, Chatsworth. Reproduced by permission of the Chatsworth Settlement Trustees)

Completed in 1814 the Italian Garden was one of the earliest revivals of the formal gardens of the 17th century with their flower-filled rectangular beds. Formal gardens had gone out of fashion due to the 18th-century vogue for landscaped gardens, pioneered by William Kent at Chiswick. However, by 1814 formal gardens were becoming popular again, as people were anxious to show off the new plants being

---

10 The pedestals on these vases are stamped `Coade Sealy Lambeth, 1801' so they may have been purchased by the 5th Duke of Devonshire and placed elsewhere in the gardens before coming to the Italian Garden. The originals are now inside the Conservatory with replicas (cast in the early 1990s) on the Conservatory steps. Spandrels and roundels on the Classic Bridge are also made from Coade Stone.

introduced into England. Formal gardens were defined by their nationalistic style: `French', `Dutch', `English' and `Italian'.

The garden's semi-circular design related to the dimensions of the Conservatory with a central axis dividing the two parts. The beds were laid out in geometric patterns, with some cut into grass, others in gravel with box edges. Some of the larger and central beds were raised a foot or so above the rest. Dotted around the garden were terms and other sculptures. There were also eight flask-type urns decorated with garlands, reminiscent of those by William Kent, and some plain vases filled with scarlet pelargoniums and other summer plants.

Fed up with the prying eyes of passers-by, the Duke rerouted Burlington Lane in 1814 to take the road further away from the house. This did not require a separate Act of Parliament, as stated in several local history books. It was made possible by the Chiswick Enclosure Act of 1814 and actually carried out under the General Highways Act of 1773 and needed the approval of two Justices of the Peace. He removed the massive iron entrance gates to give the house a less confined appearance and re-located the forecourt piers. The new entrance to Chiswick House was made opposite what is now Corney Road. This entrance had gates and a small lodge which was enlarged or completely re-designed by Decimus Burton sometime before 1848.[11]

In 1821 the Duke laid out a new northern carriageway to his estate. This is the road known today as Duke's Avenue. It was formerly the Duke's private road, with an entrance to the Horticultural Gardens (see below) on the right and then to Chiswick House.[12] In 1837 the Duke bought new wrought iron gates for this entrance. They had originally been the gates to Heathfield House, a large Chiswick residence which had just been demolished. They were painted white and gilt and ornamented with the Devonshire crest. The two sphinxes from the Forecourt were placed on the gate piers. In 1897 the 8th Duke of Devonshire removed these gates and their piers to Devonshire House in Piccadilly. When that house was demolished in 1925 the gates, with their piers and sphinxes, were bought for the nation and erected in Green Park where they remain today at the Piccadilly entrance to the park.

A new North Lodge was built at the Duke's new entrance. This is possibly the building erected by George Woolcott, builder, who was paid £533 in 1833. Purchases for the `New Lodge' such as an `Iron Bedstead' are recorded in 1837 and George Player was paid £33.19s 8d for `painting the lodge', in 1839.[13]

The Duke also put up a rectangular stone building next to the stable block. This was built onto an existing outbuilding. It is probably the building referred to thus by

---

11 According to the obituary of Decimus Burton which appeared in *The Builder*, 24th December 1881, 780 Burton designed a lodge and gates at Chiswick, garden buildings at Chatsworth, a hall and staircase at Devonshire House and made alterations to Corney House, Sutton Court and Grove House, all for the Duke of Devonshire between 1833 and 1848.

12 This road replaced a footpath from Turnham Green to Chiswick. This footpath was a public right of way and the Horticultural Society, which began negotiating its Chiswick lease in 1821, objected to a footpath running through its grounds. This may have been a contributory factor in the decision to construct Duke's Avenue.

13 Chatsworth Archives: Expenditure on Building: Repairs and Alterations

Fig 39. The gates the 6th Duke of Devonshire bought for the Duke's Avenue entrance to Chiswick House. They are now the gates from Piccadilly to Green Park (Chiswick House and Gardens Trust)

John Britton in 1816: `many sleeping rooms for the accommodation of visitors have been constructed in a detached building of considerable extent on the eastern side [of Chiswick House]'.[14]

The Duke also acquired two of Chiswick's large houses. In 1830 he bought Corney House (see p.12) which he demolished two years later. In 1854 *The Pictorial Handbook of London* claims the site was `used as a bathing place'.[15] In 1833 the Duke purchased The Grove (see p.12). It was known for its splendid Spanish chestnut trees `the magnitude and grandeur of which are probably nowhere surpassed'.[16] Some of these trees still stand today in the gardens of Hartington Road and on the Polytechnic sports ground. The Duke carried out extensive alterations to the Grove, removing the top storey entirely. The development known today as Grove Park was built on its grounds, but the house itself remained until 1928.

At some point before 1845 the Duke made a cutting across Duke's Meadows from the southern end of the Lake to the Thames to channel the flow of water and to allow water to flood into the Lake from the river at high tide. This cutting, known as Duke's Ditch, may have been along the line of an old tidal creek. He also built a brick bridge, 25ft wide, to straddle the Bollo Brook where it flowed out of his grounds.[17]

---

14 John Britton and others *The Beauties of England*, 1816, 316
15 John Weale *The Pictorial Handbook of London*, 1854, 507
16 *Ibid*, 508
17 *Report of the Committee of Magistrates appointed to make enquiries respecting the Public Bridges in the County of Middlesex*, 1826, 191

Horticultural Society Gardens

The Horticultural Society (it did not receive its Royal Charter until 1861) had been formed in 1804 by a group of eminent horticulturalists including Joseph Banks and John Wedgwood, son of the potter Josiah. In 1822 the Society leased 33 acres of land from the 6th Duke to use as an experimental garden. A private gate (the small gate within the wall from the car park to the Walled Gardens) was installed to allow the Duke (who was made President of the Society in 1838) to enter the gardens whenever he pleased.

Fig 40. A fête in the Horticultural Society Gardens in 1840 (Peter & Carolyn Hammond)

In 1827 the Society organised the first of its fêtes which were the forerunners of the Chelsea Flower Show. The fêtes became one of the main events of the London `season' with carriages to Turnham Green lining the road from Hyde Park Corner. A chapter in Anthony Trollope's *The Three Clerks*, 1858, is set in the Chiswick Gardens.

By the 1840s the Society was holding three fêtes a year and at the last (July) show, the Duke allowed visitors into Chiswick House grounds. A writer in a publication called *The Visitor* in 1848 describes the scene:

> Long, continuous files of two or three abreast passed along the walls of the kitchen garden which appeared to be very productive…the scene on the lawn in front of Chiswick House was imposing in the extreme – for there, young people were amusing themselves in rolling to and fro… the duke with a few immediate friends around him, occupying a conspicuous place, and evidently much enjoying the gratification to which he had so largely contributed.[18]

Visitors on exhibition days were also able to amuse themselves with Indian canoes on the Lake and hammocks and swings suspended amongst the trees in the Grove.

---

18 `Visit to the Chiswick Gardens' *The Visitor or Monthly Instructor for 1848*, Religious Tract Society, 365

It was in the Horticultural Gardens that the Duke met Joseph Paxton who was to become both his friend and his gardener at Chatsworth, also his adviser on the Chiswick House gardens. Paxton joined the Horticultural Gardens as a labourer in November 1823 and educated himself in the extensive Horticultural Society library. It was a good time to be a trainee gardener as the mania for plant hunting was underway and new plants like the fuchsia from Mexico, the petunia and salvia from South America, the aspidistra from China and conifers from North America were introduced in the early years of the 19th century. Paxton encountered the Duke in the Chiswick gardens and in 1826 was offered the appointment of Superintendent of the gardens of Chatsworth. He was not quite 23 years old. The Duke's money and Paxton's skill combined to turn Chatsworth into one of the most famous gardens in the kingdom and Paxton's experiments with large glasshouses culminated in his design for the Crystal Palace in 1851.[19]

Chiswick House and gardens in the early 19th century

The Duke employed John Gregory Crace (1809-1889) to re-decorate the interior of the house.[20] John Gregory was the son of Frederick Crace who was responsible for the interiors of the Royal Pavilion, Brighton so perhaps, not surprisingly, the Chiswick House décor was extravagant. In the dining room, for example, the panels were of white silk, with painted and gilt appliqué decoration, and every inch of the walls, floor and ceiling covered with ornament. The Duke described the room as a mixture between a medieval manuscript and a Parisian café.

The Duke's lavish hospitality means that several visitors have left a record of Chiswick during the Duke's tenure. A visitor in 1851 tells us that `a very charming effect is realised on the west side of the house by having two windows in the basement story formed with mirrors, in one sheet. In these the whole of the house and the cedars are most clearly reflected'.[21] The Duke also replaced the original sashes of the Venetian windows with plate glass and removed the outside staircase to the garden.

The Cedars of Lebanon were now mature and received many compliments. The writer of an article in the *Country Gentleman's Companion* said they were the most remarkable cedars he had ever seen: `I have seen as large trees, but none that had their branches so close to the ground , spreading over and covering so large a space'[22]. Other trees noted were a Cork tree, `a fine looking Lucomb Oak', `an aged specimen of the Judas tree' and `a noble specimen of the Eastern Plane Tree'. It was nearly 100ft high with branches covering a space 90ft in diameter. Attached to the tree was a tablet recording the visit of Princess Maria Nicholaevna of Russia in 1853. The Cork, Judas and Oriental Plane have now gone but the Lucomb (Fulham) oak still remains.

---

19 Sally Jeffery `Fox's "Extraordinarily Fine" Chiswick Garden', *Brentford & Chiswick Local History Journal*, No 15, 2006, 26

20 Megan Aldrick, ed, *The Craces: Royal Decorators 1768-1899; Chiswick House Account 1824-1846, Chatsworth Archives*

21 Edward Kemp *The Parks, Gardens etc of London and its Suburbs*, 1851, 105

22 T Appleby `The Duke of Devonshire's Villa at Chiswick', *Country Gentleman's Companion*, November 13th 1855, 109

Fig 41. The front of Chiswick House in 1829 by JP Neale
(Chiswick House and Gardens Trust)

Bay trees and cypresses were planted on the terraces of the Orange Tree Garden and its circular pool was filled with `aquatic plants and myriads of gold and silver fish'[23]. Black swans, which apparently bred freely at Chiswick, adorned the lake. Chamomile grew amongst the grass of the lawn, giving off a pleasant perfume when walked upon. It meant the lawn always looked green, even in the driest of summers.

It was the heyday of plant collecting and the Duke was not slow to introduce new species to Chiswick. Rhododendrons were planted bordering the Serpentine Walk and in 1828 the Duke replaced the peaches, figs and vines grown in the Conservatory with Camellias (at the time it was thought that such exotic flowers could only be grown in hot houses). The Chiswick House camellia collection is perhaps the oldest of its type in the country and contains some very rare varieties including Middlemist's Red, thought to be only one of two in the world, and other varieties which have not been identified.

The Conservatory was described in 1851 as having a dome, `part of which is glazed with stained glass and crowned with a gilt ornament' [24] (the dome was completely remodelled in 1933, altered again in 1990 and rebuilt in 2009). *The Cottage Gardener* in 1855 reported that the old fashioned small glass in the hot houses was being replaced with long squares of `best glass'. Large glass panels were just coming onto the market at the time; they increased the quality and quantity of light and reduced maintenance.

---

23 Edward Kemp *see above*, 110
24 *Ibid*

Also in 1855, the hypocaust heating system was abandoned and converted to a system of gravity-piped hot water fed by boilers in pits at the end of each of the back sheds.

The Duke's new Conservatory meant that the former Orangery (see p.37) was redundant. The roof was removed to form what came to be known as the Arcade – five arches, surmounted by an entablature and balustrade with Corinthian columns and a pebbled mosaic floor. Backed with high yew hedges and curving paths, this formed an archway between the Duke's old and new gardens. The Arcade building was demolished sometime before 1892 but its ornamental pebbled floor remains, covered by a raised platform. Outside the Arcade was an octagonal stone basin with a fountain in the centre which `has a variety of jets so as to be capable of being played in several forms'.[25]

Walter Scott in his diary entry for 17th May 1828 says `I drove down to Chiswick where I had not been before. A numerous and gay party were assembled to walk in and enjoy the beauty of that Palladian House'. The poet William Wordsworth apparently `enjoyed the scene intensely' when he visited in 1836.

Fig 42. The Arcade building in 1845. Originally Lord Burlington's Orangery, it now formed an archway between the 6th Duke of Devonshire's old and new gardens (Local Studies, Chiswick Library)

In a letter dated 1843 the Duke's sister, Harriet Granville (Haryo) wrote: 'Chiswick, dearest brother, Chiswick! What shall I say? Chatsworth be jealous'. Harriet goes on to record the impressions of first time visitor Charles Greville:

> `it was an utter surprise. He said he had never seen anything so pretty than your room! The Carpets, the improvements in the garden, the walk through the open room to the

25 *Ibid*, 107

Horticultural, the flowers, the perfect enamel of the parterre, the pink passion flower, Landseer's pictures. Charles Greville fell from astonishment to astonishment..."God bless my soul. Have you seen anything abroad to compare with Chiswick?"[26]

The Duke's diary entries show that he was also fond of Chiswick: `At Chiswick all day. It is irresistible in this weather' (June 1835); `Enjoying too much the delicious indolence of Chiswick' (June 1838); `It is an enchantment at Chiswick' (April 1857).

The menagerie

An additional attraction for visitors to Chiswick House during the time of the Duke was the opportunity to inspect the creatures in his menagerie. Menageries were the forerunners of zoos, but they had nothing to do with conservation, research or environmental education; they were just a way for Royalty and the aristocracy to demonstrate their wealth. Menageries were known from medieval times; King John set one up at the Tower of London in the 12th century and George IV maintained a royal menagerie in Windsor Great Park. Animals from these two menageries were transferred to the newly-opened London Zoo in the 1830s. There were also travelling menageries in the 18th and 19th centuries. These `Wild Beast Shows' gave people in the provinces their first glimpse of exotic animals.

The accounts for Chiswick House, kept in the Chatsworth Archive, show that the Duke made regular payments for food for an elephant, birds (these included a cockatoo and gold and silver pheasants) and a monkey.[27] We know from other sources that the menagerie also contained a llama, elks, emus, kangaroos, ostriches, a Neapolitan pig, goats `of all colours and dimensions', `an Indian bull and his spouse'[28], a coatimundi (a member of the racoon family) and `a dear little creature called an ichneumon who was apt to drop on the back of one's neck during dinner and had a propensity for sucking human blood...'[29] The menagerie building was sited on a grassy mound just north of the Classic Bridge, according to articles written during the 19th century.

In October 1820 the Duke's sister Harriet wrote to their sister Georgiana:

> He [the 6th Duke] is improving Chiswick most amazingly, opening and airing it and a delightful walk is made around the paddock, open and dry, with a view of Kew Palace – and a few kangaroos (who if affronted rip up a body as soon as look at him), elks, emus and other pretty sportive death dealers playing around near it.[30]

Harriet, obviously with some relief, writes to her sister the following month: `... I own I think it a mercy that one of the kangaroos has just died in labour, vu that they might hug one to death.'[31]

---

26 Quoted in Virginia Surtees (ed) *A Second Self: the Letters of Harriet Granville 1810-1846*, 1990

27 Chatsworth & Devonshire MSS Chiswick and Brighton Household Accounts, 1824-1846

28 Warwick Draper *Chiswick*, [1923] 1973 edition, 118

29 Quoted in Betty Askwith *Piety and Wit, a Biography of Harriet Countess of Granville* 1982, 123

30 Quoted in Virginia Surtees *see above*, 145

31 *Ibid*

The spitting llama also failed to impress Prince Pückler-Muskau, who visited Chiswick House in 1826:

> The llama, the size of a hind, has no other weapon than to spit very bad smelling saliva at people. It is very angry and when forced in any way will do its manoeuvre, which looks very ridiculous. Nonetheless one has to watch out because it spits with vehemence and hits the mark'.[32]

The star of the Duke's menagerie was undoubtedly Sadi the large Indian elephant. *The Library of Entertaining Knowledge* suggests this is how the elephant was acquired:

> The Duke of Devonshire, having been asked by a lady of rank what she should send him from India, and having laughingly answered, "Oh, nothing smaller than an elephant", was surprised to find, at the expiration of some months, a very handsome female of the species consigned to his care.[33]

If this anecdote is true the `lady of rank' must have been the wife of the Marquis of Hastings who, according to the *Morning Chronicle* in 1818, supplied the Duke with his elephant, although a reference to an elephant keeper at Chiswick House in the Chatsworth archives for 1811 suggests the elephant was there by that date. References differ as to whether the elephant was male or female, most suggest the latter.

The elephant was noted by Prince Pückler-Muskau on his 1826 visit: `There is a menagerie attached to the garden, in which a tame elephant performs all sorts of feats and very quietly suffers anybody to ride him about a large lawn'[34].

And again by Walter Scott in his diary entry for 1828: `... the scene was dignified by the presence of an immense elephant, who under the charge of a groom wandered up and down, giving an air of Asiatic pageantry to the entertainment'[35].

The elephant was apparently:

> Kept in a house of large dimensions, well ventilated and arranged in every particular with a proper regard to the comfort of the animal. But she often had the range of a spacious paddock; and the exhibition of her sagacity was therefore doubly pleasing, for it was evidently not effected by rigid confinement'.[36]

Sadi had a number of party tricks:

> We remember seeing him some years ago perform a variety of manoeuvres at the word of command. When told to dress himself, he would take down a scarlet cloak from a peg

---

32 Flora Brennan (trans) *Pücklers Progress: the Adventures of Prince Pückler-Muskau in England, Wales and Ireland told in Letters to his former wife 1826-7*, 1986, 26
33 `The Menageries, quadrupeds described and drawn from living sources', *The Library of Entertaining Knowledge*, 1831, 7
34 Flora Brennan (trans) *see above*
35 The Journal of Sir Walter Scott, ed Anderson 1998, 534
36 `Menageries, quadrupeds etc' *see above*, 7

and throw it with a jaunty air over his ample shoulders; and then kneel down for any of the spectators to mount for a ride; after which he would replace his cloak, take up a bucket and fetch it full of water from the river, and seizing a broom or a scrubbing-brush, would begin cleaning his house'.[37]

The elephant was also able to uncork a tightly-stoppered soda water bottle, tip the contents into its trunk, and then into its mouth without spilling a drop. Sadi died in 1829 when she/he was about 21 years-old, apparently from pulmonary consumption.

The Chiswick menagerie was transferred to Chatsworth, probably in 1836 when the `Dogs and Waterfowl' food accounts cease but a new set of Chatsworth payments for animal food begin.

Entertainments

The Duke held some lavish parties at Chiswick House. In 1814 he entertained Emperor Alexander I of Russia, the King of Prussia, Marshall Blücher with `many illustrious persons in attendance on these monarchs'. In 1847 he threw a party for his Imperial Highness the Grand Duke Constantine of Russia, and in 1842 Her Majesty herself with Prince Albert, and many other members of the Royal Family, attended a fête.

Fig 43. The Summer Parlour flying the Imperial Standard at the Duke's fête for the Tsar of Russia in 1844 as pictured in the Illustrated London News (Local Studies, Chiswick Library)

Most celebrated of all, though, was the fête the Duke held in June1844 in honour of the visit to Britain by Emperor Nicholas I of Russia. Apart from the Tsar, it was attended by the King of Saxony, Prince Albert and around 700 members of the principal noble families in the land and described as `one of the most splendid fêtes ever given in this country'.[38]

---

37 `Walks in the Neighbourhood of London', *The London Saturday Journal*, November 1839, 296
38 William Keane *The Beauties of Middlesex*, 1850, 222

The royal cavalcade entered the gates of Chiswick House at five minutes to two, preceded by outriders in state liveries. On their arrival, the Imperial Standard was raised over the Summer Parlour and the Royal Standard over the Arcade and a 21-gun salute fired from a battery erected within the grounds. The bands of the Coldstream Guards and the Horse Guards simultaneously played the Russian national anthem. After a tour round the house, the Tsar and 16 other important guests adjourned to the Summer Parlour which was fitted out like a 14th-century military pavilion where they dined off silver plate. To commemorate his visit, Emperor Nicholas planted a cedar deodar tree in front of the house to replace a cedar tree that had been blown down.

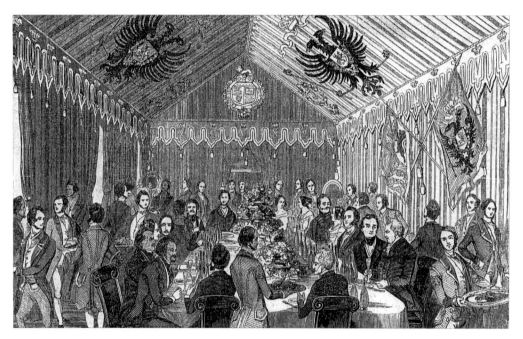

Fig 44. Banquet held in the Summer Parlour for the Tsar of Russia in 1844
(Local Studies, Chiswick Library)

After the `dejeuner', the royal party retired to the lawn. Here four giraffes were conspicuously on display and seem to have provided plenty of entertainment. According to an account of the fête in the *Illustrated London News*:

> The company dispersed in groups about the grounds – some few, among whom was the King of Saxony and his attendants, crossing the lake in boats manned by the duke's watermen in their state liveries, for the purpose of inspecting the giraffes, which were on the opposite shore. Before the King's arrival, however, one of these animals waded across the water and joined the company; an incident which amused the Royal party.[39]

---

39 `The Duke of Devonshire's grand fête for the Emperor of Russia at Chiswick House',
   Illustrated London News 15th June, 1844, 386

These animals, though, probably did not belong to the Duke (the menagerie had already been transferred to Chatsworth). Carl Gustav Carus who chronicled the King of Saxony's visit to the fête writes that he was told that the Duke had only hired the giraffes for a day from `a man who had them for show'.[40] The *Illustrated London News* article said that the giraffes came from the Surrey Zoological Gardens and were about to be shipped to St Petersburg. The Duke was one of the subscribers to the Surrey Zoo which had acquired five giraffes in 1843 but was only advertising one in 1845.

THE TEMPLE LAWN, WITH THE EXHIBITION OF THE GIRAFFES.

Fig 45. The giraffes in Chiswick House gardens at the fête given by the 6th Duke of Devonshire for the Tsar of Russia in 1844 from the Illustrated London News *(Local Studies, Chiswick Library)*

The giraffes were probably those kept in a giraffe house and paddock where Upham Park Road is today, just north of Chiswick High Road, opposite Chiswick Lane.

There is good evidence for the giraffe house; it is shown on local maps and mentioned in the Chiswick rate books. There is also this visual memory from Jessie McGregor writing in 1918 about her childhood:

> When I was walking with my mother or nurse, we often remarked with curiosity, a large and somewhat dilapidated wooden building, standing in a bit of waste ground, not a quarter of a mile from the place I now know Chiswick House to be....Painted on the wall in large letters more than half effaced by time and weather were scrawled the mysterious words "Four Giraffes". When I first read of the giraffes at Chiswick House, it was impossible not to connect one circumstance with the other, and to wonder whether the wooden shed with the unexplained legend on the wall, could possibly have been that which, once upon a time, had sheltered the queer-looking animals, provided by the Duke of Devonshire for the Czar's entertainment'.[41]

---

40 Carl Gustav Carus *The King of Saxony's Journey through England and Scotland*, 1846, 93
41 Jessie McGregor *Gardens of Celebrities and Celebrated Gardens in and around London*, 1918, 186

Giraffes would be a strange sight in Chiswick even today, so it would be odd if the giraffes kept in the Chiswick giraffe house were not the same as those displayed by the Duke of Devonshire. Perhaps they were kept on the Upham Park Road plot by `the man who had them for show', mentioned by Carus, or perhaps the giraffe house was just a temporary arrangement for the Duke's party.

The bachelor Duke died in January 1858, aged 67, at Hardwick Hall. His death was unexpected. He had seemed well the previous day when he went out in his carriage but was found dead in bed the next morning.

Chapter 6

RELATIONS AND TENANTS (1858-1929)

Lady Granville (1858-1862)

The Bachelor Duke was succeeded as 7th Duke of Devonshire by William Cavendish, the grandson of George Cavendish, the third son of the 4th Duke and Charlotte Boyle. He was thus Hart's cousin once removed.

The 6th Duke left a legacy of £1,600 to Joseph Paxton, and Chiswick House to his elder sister, Georgiana (little G), now Lady Carlisle, for her lifetime. Unfortunately she died only seven months after the Duke, so the life interest in Chiswick passed to Harriet (Haryo), the Duke's younger sister. She alternated between Chiswick and her house in Mayfair for the last four years of her life.

Harriet had married Lord Granville at Chiswick on 24 December 1809. It was an odd match. Not only was Granville 12 years older than Harriet but he had been carrying on a long-term affair with Harriet's aunt, Lady Bessborough, by whom he had two children. The marriage, though, was happy and produced five children. Harriet also adopted the two offspring of Lord Granville and Lady Bessborough. Lord Granville did several stints as British Ambassador to France in the 1820s and 1830s when Harriet acted as society hostess to the cosmopolitan Parisian society.

On the Duke's death, his steward William Currey had sent Harriet's son a broad brush estimate of £2,946 for the running of Chiswick House and grounds. Currey confirmed that Harriet would receive £4,000 a year from the Devonshire Estate and that, in addition, she would receive rent of £1,800 a year from the Chiswick estate, some of which was leased out.

The 1861 Census records the following people at Chiswick on the night of 7th April: Harriet herself, her son Frederick Leveson Gower (aged 41 and widowed) and his two-year old son, George. These three were living at Chiswick. Visiting were Susan, Gertrude and Constance Pitt, Harriet's granddaughters, the children of her daughter, Susan; George A Stuart who is almost certainly George Stewart the illegitimate son of Granville's liaison with Lady Bessborough; Francis Osborne, second son of the Duke of Leeds, his wife and six year old daughter. There was also a governess called Jane Doggett and 24 indoor servants (some of these would have been visitors' servants). Two coachmen, a groom and a lodge-keeper are listed as outdoor servants.

Haryo, once a lively person and witty letter writer, became something of a recluse after her husband died in 1846. Like her brother, she embraced religion and she devoted herself to philanthropy. According to her son `she wished to sell camellias from the Conservatory in order to give the proceeds to charity, but she had some misgivings as to whether she was justified in doing so'. No one apparently raised any objections and she wrote to a friend `Dear me, how rich my poor will be'.

Lady Granville occupied two small rooms in one of the wings, leaving the rest of the house to be enjoyed by her children and grandchildren. Her son tells us that she found the library a great resource and that she `dined apart but we alternately joined her after dinner'.[1]

In 1861 a fête to raise funds for the West London Hospital, Hammersmith was held in the Chiswick House gardens (admission 1/-). Sadly two people drowned in the lake at this event. Lady Granville also granted a request from the Friendly Societies in Hammersmith to celebrate their annual holiday in the Chiswick grounds, despite the misgivings of her gardener. Her son's memoirs record that:

> Some five thousand people, men, women and children arrived, and it enchanted my
> mother to peep from behind her window curtains and see so many happy faces…
> Beyond trampling down the grass this large crowd did no damage.[2]

Harriet's son held a very grand social event at Chiswick in 1862, reported in *The Times* and headlined `The Earl Granville's Fête at Chiswick'. `The company began to arrive at three, and carriages continued to set down until nearly six o'clock. The company altogether numbered nearly 2,000 persons, and included their Royal Highnesses the Duchess of Cambridge and Princess Mary of Cambridge.'[3] Other members of the Royal Family were present as well as various ambassadors, members of the aristocracy and notables such as William Makepeace Thackeray. Earl Granville was Chairman of the International Exhibition which had opened on 1 May in Kensington and was a successor to the Great Exhibition of 1851. The fête was held to celebrate the opening of the exhibition. At another evening party at Chiswick, the gardens were illuminated by 200 Chinese lanterns and there was also a band, `Bengal lights' [fireworks] and other attractions.

The Duchess of Sutherland (1863-1868)

After Lady Granville's death in 1862 the 7th Duke of Devonshire offered Chiswick House to one of Lady Granville's nephews, who declined it, then to Harriet Howard, Dowager Duchess of Sutherland, Lady Granville's niece, the eldest daughter of her sister Georgiana and the 6th Earl of Carlisle.

Harriet Howard, born in 1806, had married at the age of 17 Earl Gower, her cousin and 20 years her senior. The marriage produced 12 children. In 1833, on the death of his father, Earl Gower inherited the title Duke of Sutherland.

The Sutherlands were enormously wealthy. Their town house Stafford House (now Lancaster House) overlooks Green Park and they also owned Trentham Hall in Staffordshire, Lilleshall Hall in Shropshire, Dunrobin Castle in Sutherland and

---

1   Frederick Leveson Gower *Bygone Years: Recollections*, 1905
2   *Ibid*
3   *The Times*, 2nd June 1862

the Cliveden Estate by the Thames, which they rebuilt after a fire. Queen Victoria is supposed to have said on a visit to the Duchess `I have come from my house to your palace'.[4] The Duchess was appointed Mistress of the Robes when Victoria came to the throne in 1837. This was a political appointment, with each government having the right to change the personnel, so the duchess was in and out over the next 25 years, depending on the fortunes of the Whig party. But it appears that Queen Victoria valued her company and she was one of the only people outside the Queen's family who was a welcome companion just after the death of Prince Albert.

The Duchess had been widowed for two years before she came to Chiswick where she lived intermittently for the last five years of her life. She split her time between Stafford House in London, Cliveden and Chiswick, which she had been offered rent free but with the Duchess responsible for the total upkeep of the estate.

She seems to have kept her side of this bargain very well, judging from the ledgers of Chiswick builder Henry Eydmann. Eydmann did a great deal of work in the district and for many years his firm did all the building, repairs and decoration at Chiswick House. During the tenure of the Duchess, he carried out minor tasks from repairing locks to moving garden furniture, spring cleaning the house and making boxes for transferring produce from one house to another. More major jobs were repairing the top of the Conservatory and carrying out extensive plumbing work in 1864. This involved excavating the outside drains, putting in new soil pipes and cleaning out cesspools. The ledgers show that in 1865 Eydmann built a wine cellar for the Duchess. This is perhaps the 19th-century addition to an earlier vault found during excavations in 2008 on the site where the café has now been built.[5]

Shortly after she moved to Chiswick, the Duchess held a garden party on 7th July 1863 which was reported in *The Times*: `Their Royal Highnesses the Prince and Princess of Wales honoured the Dowager Duchess of Sutherland by their presence at an afternoon party, at her Grace's beautiful villa at Chiswick'. The party began at 4pm and the royal guests left at 7pm.[6]

The Duchess also hosted a visit from the Italian military and political hero Giuseppe Garibaldi. The Duchess had always been interested in public affairs; she was a friend of Gladstone with whom she carried on a correspondence and who visited her in Chiswick. In the 1860s she made known her support for Garibaldi and the cause of Italian unification.

Garibaldi was entertained for lunch at Chiswick House on 12th April 1864. He arrived in an open barouche to the sound of the band of the 2nd Life Guards playing the Garibaldi hymn – they played it again when he left. He was escorted to the centre salon to meet the company and was then taken to the `summer dining room' where covers were laid for 20 people. After lunch Garibaldi was taken around the gardens

---

4   Quoted in K D Reynolds `The Duchess of Sutherland', *Oxford Dictionary of National Biography*, 2004

5   David Fellows `This Old House: Excavations at Chiswick House', *Current Archaeology*, October 2008, 28

6   *The Times*, July 1863

where he planted a commemorative tree, a deodar cedar, on the lawn in front of the house.[7]

The Duchess also allowed Chiswick to be used for a charitable event in 1864, a sale of jewellery `offered by Polish ladies of all ranks', the proceeds were to go to the sick and wounded in Poland, victims of the country's struggle to achieve independence from Russia. The gardens were open to the public between 2pm and 7pm, admission price 5d.[8]

When the Duchess died on 27th October 1868 Gladstone recorded in his journal: `The post brought a black bordered letter which announced the death of the Dowager Duchess of Sutherland. I have lost in her from view the warmest and dearest friend, surely, that ever man had'.[9] He acted as one of the pallbearers at her funeral several days later.

The Prince of Wales (1869-1877)

By January 1869, the Prince of Wales (later King Edward VII) had taken over the lease on Chiswick House. At the time the Prince and Princess had four children: Prince Albert, Prince George, Princess Louise and Princess Victoria, ranging in age from five years to five months. In December 1869 another daughter, Princess Maud was born (a sixth child, Prince John, born in 1871 died the same year). Chiswick House was used as both a summer nursery for the children and a place where the Prince could hold outdoor entertainments; his London home, Marlborough House, having only a small garden and his estate at Sandringham being too far away from town.

Queen Victoria did not approve. She wrote to her son in 1869: `There is a great fear lest you should have gay parties at Chiswick instead of going there to pass the Sunday, a day which is rightly considered one of rest, quietly for your repose with your dear children'.[10]

Since the press in those days had a greater respect for the privacy of the Royal Family, there is very little information about the Prince's tenure of Chiswick House.

It is hard to see anyway how the Royal Family were able to spend much time at Chiswick, even in the summer, as their usual round was to go to Sandringham, then move on to Osborne Lodge on the Isle of Wight for the Cowes Regatta and transfer to Abergeldie on the Balmoral estate in the late summer.

We do know that when at Chiswick the children were often joined by their cousins, the children of the Duke and Duchess of Teck who lived in White Lodge, Richmond. The eldest Teck daughter, Victoria Mary, known as May, was to marry the future King George V in 1893. The children sometimes travelled to see their grandmother at Windsor Castle, returning to Chiswick on the South Western Railway.

---

7   *Ibid*, 13th April, 1864

8   *Ibid*, 14th May, 1864, 10

9   Quoted in HCG Matthew (ed) *The Gladstone Diaries*, 1978

10 Quoted in Georgiana Battiscombe, *Queen Alexandra*, 1969

Each child was allocated a small plot of ground to cultivate in the Chiswick House gardens. Later known as the `Princes' Garden' or the `Royal Garden' the plots were by the Inigo Jones Gateway where the café is today. This garden continued to be cultivated long after the children had left. In 1933 when the Council had taken over responsibility for the upkeep of the gardens, they recommended the demolition of the stable block/Grosvenor Wing `subject to steps being taken for the protection of the gardens of the princes in the vicinity'. The garden was photographed as late as 1948, still well tended and with the name of each Royal child on the different plots.

Fig 46. The plots set aside for the children of the Prince of Wales, each bearing the name of the prince or princess who tended it. The plots were still being cultivated when this photo was taken in 1948.
(Chiswick House and Gardens Trust)

According to an 1869 entry in the 7th Duke of Devonshire's journal, the Prince was to have Chiswick on the same terms as the Duchess of Sutherland, in other words rent free but with responsibility for the upkeep. The Prince continued to use the firm of Henry Eydmann for maintenance but, unfortunately, Eydmann's ledgers only cover the first 18 months of the Prince's tenure, during which time Eydmann prepared the house for the arrival of the family's visits and undertook small jobs such as whitewashing and repairing flashings. Presumably no major work was needed as the Duchess had left the place in such good shape. Because the Prince had his own large sources of supply, he let out the kitchen garden and the park. The Prince also appears to have brought his own servants to Chiswick as the 1871 census lists only two lodge keepers, a gardener, a housekeeper and two maids at Chiswick House the day the census was taken.

The garden seems to have been well tended. When a journalist from the *Journal of Horticulture and Cottage Gardener* visited in 1874, no fewer than 13,000 bedding plants were ready to be put out.

Thanks to reports in *The Times* newspaper, we know about the brilliant garden parties the Prince held at Chiswick. Apart from his first year there, he normally held at least one party a year and two in each of the years 1870-1873. The parties were variously called dejeuners, breakfasts or garden parties; they started in the late afternoon and finished mid evening. Everybody who was anybody attended and the Queen sometimes put in an appearance. She travelled to Chiswick from Windsor by a special train and was escorted to and from the station by a detachment of the 1st Life Guards. However, a letter to her eldest daughter in July 1875 suggests she was not overly enamoured:

You say that Bertie's breakfast must have been charming. I myself think them dreadful and very fatiguing bores, walking and standing about and seeing fresh faces in every direction – but it doesn't last long and pleases people and so there it is and easily done'.[11]

The Prince's most famous party was one given in honour of the Shah of Persia who visited England in 1873. The party on the 28th June was recorded thus in *The Times*: `

On Saturday afternoon the Shah went to the Prince of Wales's Garden Party at Chiswick. From Buckingham Palace to the gates of the Duke of Devonshire's beautiful villa the route was crowded. Her Majesty honoured the party with her presence, the gardens were in their fullest beauty and the long list which we publish will show that "everybody" was there.[12] (The list filled nearly three columns of the paper.)

Fig 47. The Shah of Persia at the garden party at Chiswick House given by the Prince and Princess of Wales in July 1873, as depicted in the Illustrated London News *(Chiswick House and Gardens Trust)*

The Shah's visit was a `red-letter day for Chiswick', according to a local gentleman writing about it 60 years later:

The whole district was en fête for the occasion. The well-known song "Have you seen the Shah?" was a sequel to the Persian ruler's visit, and I remember Chiswick boys whistling it all day long…all the notables of England gathered at Chiswick House to

---

11 Quoted in Christopher Hibbert *Queen Victoria in her Letters and Journals: a Selection*, 1984
12 *The Times*, 30th June, 1873, 11

welcome the Shah, and carriages in a single line stretched from Kensington to Chiswick. Seats to view the long procession were easily sold for 2s to 10s each'.[13]

Also staying with the Queen at Windsor were the Tsarevitch (the future Emperor Alexander III of Russia) and his wife. Prior to attending the fête for the Shah the Tsarevitch visited Messrs Thornycroft's works by St Nicholas Church, Chiswick to inspect the fast steamers being built there. He was given a ride in a fast boat called the *Miranda* and apparently: 'cooled down' by his blow on the river' (it was an extremely hot day) 'danced with much zeal and activity to the inspiring music of the gipsy band'.[14]

'A Royal Garden party at Chiswick' was the subject of a very large picture by Louis William Desanges. Measuring 16ft by 7ft, it included 300 figures with Queen Victoria and the Prince of Wales taking centre stage. The Prince and his family sat for Desanges in 1875 but the painting was not ready for the Royal Academy Summer Exhibition in 1876. It was exhibited at the premises of the Autotype Company in 1879. But, sadly in November of that year, it was completely destroyed when escaping gas caused a massive fire. There is, though, an autotype (an early form of photographic reproduction) version of it in Chiswick House.

Fig 48. The Shah planting a cedar tree to commemorate his visit in 1873 (Chiswick House and Gardens Trust)

Several of the Prince's distinguished guests commemorated their visit by planting a tree in the gardens. In 1873 the Shah of Persia planted a *Wellingtonia gigantean*, as did the Tsarevitch while the Tsarina planted a *Salisburia adiantofolia*. Cedars of Lebanon were planted in 1874 by Queen Victoria, the Prince and Princess of Wales, and the Duchess of Edinburgh, another in 1876 by the King and Queen of the Hellenes.

As well as parties, the Prince gave a private dinner at Chiswick for Alexander II of Russia during his visit to England in May 1874. (This is the emperor who was assassinated in 1881.) The Prince also watched the boat race from Chiswick House in March 1873, together with his family and the Duchess of Teck.

---

13 'The High Road Sixty Years Ago', *The Chiswick Review* March 1924
14 *Freeman's Journal and Daily Commercial Advertiser* 29th July 1873

The Prince gave up his tenancy in 1877 which caused the 7th Duke of Devonshire to lament the difficulty of letting Chiswick House:

> … the Prince of Wales has given up the place, it is now on my hands and it is not easy to decide what to do with it. I do not see any probability of my ever wishing to live there. The house is in a dirty state and wants a thorough overhaul.[15]

It lay empty for the next four years although the Duke seems to have let out the gardens for various functions. In July 1878 the United Committee for Special Services (a religious association interested in the movement for providing religious services for people in theatres and music halls) held a meeting in the garden, according to a report in the *Illustrated London News*.[16]

The Marquess of Bute (1881-1892)

The Duke's next tenant was the Marquess of Bute (1847-1900). John Patrick Crichton-Stuart, 3rd Marquess of Bute, 7th Earl of Bute, Earl of Dumfries, Earl of Windsor, Viscout Mountjoy and Baron Mountstuart was a wealthy nobleman who left £2m in his will. He married in 1872 the Honourable Gwendoline Fitzjames Howard, niece of the Duke of Norfolk; the marriage produced a daughter and three sons.

The Marquess possessed several large estates - Cardiff Castle, Mountstuart, Dumfries House - but he didn't have a home in the capital. In a letter he wrote in 1873 he said: `we have no London address, neither of us caring for the place, where no one left me a house and where I have not the least intention of buying'.[17] However, by 1881 he must have seen the necessity of a London base.

The Census of 1881 shows that the Marquess lived in some style; 23 domestic servants are listed with eight staff in the stables, a gatekeeper housed in the old North Lodge,[18] a head gardener and under gardener in houses in the grounds.[19] An article in *The English Illustrated Magazine* gives a glimpse of the interior of Chiswick House:

> The large drawing room in one of the wings where some of the best pictures hang, upon the walls of painted cream-colour satin having a broad band of dark red velvet five feet from the floor, upon which are arranged miniatures, medals, seals and curious old faience.

The article also mentions that the kitchen and offices were at some distance from the living room (they were in the service building/stable block) and were connected

---

15 Journal of the 7th Duke of Devonshire, 6th June 1877 (Chatsworth Archive)

16 `A Chiswick Garden Meeting', *Illustrated London News*, 27th July 1878

17 David Hunter Blair *John Patrick, 3rd Marquess of Bute (1846-1900)*, 1921

18 This was demolished when the A4 was extended in the 1950s and replaced with the present North Lodge on the opposite side of Duke's Avenue.

19 One of these was Kent House. There appears to have been a building on that site in 1818, although its shape had been altered by the time of the 1892 Ordnance Survey map. Paxton House first appears on the 1892 map.

Fig 49. The Conservatory and Italian Garden in 1883 (Chiswick House and Gardens Trust)

by a 'most curious miniature railway which, unless time and distance are very nicely calculated, the dishes for dinner are apt to arrive at uncertain intervals'.[20]

The Marquess had been reared as a Presbyterian but at 21 years old converted to Roman Catholicism. He was a religious man, who wrote religious books, and his only known alteration to Chiswick House was the creation of a Roman Catholic Chapel in the room now known as the Gallery; the young Earl of Dumfries was christened there by the Roman Catholic Bishop of the Isles in 1881, and the Marquess's third son baptised in 1886 by Cardinal Manning. The Marquess also contributed £500 towards building the new Roman Catholic Church in Chiswick (opened 1886).

By the 19th century the Chiswick House estate was becoming truncated as the 7th Duke of Devonshire began to sell off its land for development. In 1867 plans were published for a spacious estate between the river and the railway (Chiswick Station had been opened in 1849). The Grove Park Hotel (now the Old Station House) was built in 1867 and St Paul's Church in 1872. However, few houses were put up and the rest of the area was developed later on a piecemeal basis. In 1884 the Duke drained and infilled the upper part of the Chiswick House Lake and in 1886 land bounded by Burlington Lane/Barrowgate Road/and Sutton Court Road on the west was offered for sale by auction. The estate, which comprised 125 acres at the time of the 6th Duke, was thus whittled down to its present 66 acres.

---

20 *English Illustrated Magazine*, 1888/9, 94

The Chiswick House gardens themselves appear to have been well maintained, a reporter from *Gardening World* who visited in 1887 praises the `smooth, velvety lawn dotted with the once fashionable statuary and various trees'. He mentions too that numerous laurels were planted on the terraces of the Orange Tree Garden and that orchids and stove plants (plants that require artificial heat) were growing at one end of the Conservatory, while the other contained ferns.[21] The various features of the gardens appear to have been differently named in 1889 - the Exedra (to which the Marquess constructed a new path) is `Poets Corner', the Bowling Green, `the Chestnut Square', the Orange Tree Garden, the `Bay Ground' and the Cascade, which was `draped and concealed with a mantle of ivy' was called `the Grotto'. Although his lease on Chiswick ran until 1892 the Marquess probably spent little time there after 1888 as in that year he took out a 27 year lease on St John's Lodge in Regents Park.

Fig 50. The Conservatory and Italian Garden in 2011 (© Adam Watson)

Chiswick House Asylum (1892-1928)

Perhaps the difficulty of finding tenants for Chiswick House is the reason why the 8th Duke of Devonshire allowed the building to be rented out as a mental asylum in 1892. Some say this was the nadir of Chiswick House's history. The Duke took the precaution, though, of moving most of the pictures and some of the statuary to Chatsworth, prior to, or soon after, the new tenants moved in. In 1897 the iron gates (see p56) at the Duke's Avenue entrance were removed to Devonshire House in Piccadilly. `Chiswick has just suffered a sad loss. The Duke of Devonshire has taken up his gates and walked with them to Piccadilly' lamented the *Pall Mall Gazette*.[22]

---

21 `Chiswick House', *The Gardening World*, 7th May 1887, 76
22 *Pall Mall Gazette*, 17th April 1897

Fig 51. The gates at the Duke's Avenue entrance in the early 20th century. The lion and lioness on the gate piers were brought to Chiswick by the Tuke family from their previous asylum in Chiswick Lane. They were removed from the Duke's Avenue gates when that entrance was moved back to construct the A4 and in 2004 were placed on the gate piers at Stavelely Road (Peter & Carolyn Hammond)

The Chiswick House asylum was no ordinary mental asylum, though. It was private, expensive and exclusive (some patients were titled). It was also a pioneer in the more humane treatment of the insane, relying on listening and talking to patients rather than plying them with drugs or physically restraining them.

The asylum was run by Dr Thomas Seymour Tuke and Dr Charles Molesworth Tuke whose father, Dr Harrington Tuke, had been running a mental asylum in Chiswick since 1837. This was originally housed in a large mansion called Manor House in Chiswick Lane but, by 1892, this building was about to be demolished to facilitate the widening of Chiswick Lane.

The asylum staff were understandably apprehensive about how the move would affect their vulnerable patients, as shown by the patients' case notes which are in the Wellcome Library. For one patient they read: `He is to be transferred on the 8th, but it is considered inadvisable to inform him'. You can sense a sigh of relief in the entry for the following day: `Transferred today. Went very quietly'. And in another patient's entry: ` Has been moved to Chiswick House…has not broken any windows'.

It's perhaps important to note that the Palladian villa was not part of the mental asylum, being used only by the Tuke family and for functions such as balls, fêtes and charitable events. The west wing of the house is thought to have been the home of Dr Thomas Seymour Tuke and the east wing used as a surgery, consulting room, nurses' mess room with perhaps some accommodation for staff and patients. The house's stable block/service building (Grosvenor Wing) contained between 40 and 50 rooms presumably for patients, and an adjacent building housed other patients, possibly those who posed a danger to themselves or others since it was known as the `acute wing'. Dr Charles Molesworth Tuke negotiated a separate lease with the Duke for a plot of land near the Duke's Avenue entrance. Here he built the Gatehouse as his family home (it first appears in the rate books in 1896).

The 1901 census lists 34 patients at Chiswick House asylum, evenly split between men and women. There were 48 staff at the house and other staff living in Paxton House, Kent House and the stable block. Some patients had their own suite of rooms and a staff of servants.

Fresh air and outside activities were encouraged. The 1898 report of the annual inspection of the asylum by the Commissioners in Lunacy reads that `the majority of patients were in the grounds'. When she was a child in the 1920s, Pamela Newton, whose mother was a friend of Dr Tuke, was allowed to walk in the gardens of Chiswick

Fig 52. Charles Molesworth Tuke and his youngest brother and sister (© David Tuke)

House and recollects seeing `the occasional resident, walking arm in arm with a nurse – uniformed with a long white veil'.[23] The Tukes, who were keen cricketers themselves, constructed the cricket pitch near Staveley Road and encouraged cricket matches between residents and teams from outside. There were also tennis courts, and, according to the *Chiswick Times* in 1914, a nine-hole golf course. The notes for one patient in 1915 show that he played squash most days. The squash court was probably the small, enclosed, and now derelict, space to the west of the large wrought iron gates to the Walled Gardens.[24]

---

23 Pamela Newton `Memories of Chiswick House Grounds in the 1920s', *Chiswick Parish Magazine*, May 1995, 5

24 Since the game of squash only began to be played in the early 20th century and the court at Chiswick House is shown on the 1865 Ordnance Survey map, it was probably previously used for the game of Fives. There is a wartime reference in the Brentford and Chiswick Council Minutes: `hutches for the breeding of rabbits have been installed in the old Fives Court at Chiswick House'. There is also, though, an intriguing reference to a Real Tennis Court at Chiswick House. Pamela Newton *see above* writing about the 1920s says: `Behind the Camellia House was still the high brick wall of the back of the disused Real Tennis Court. Steps led up to a small brick area from which watchers could have seen the tennis'. However, Real Tennis courts are much larger than squash or fives courts. They measure 100ft x 40ft and there is no building of these dimensions on any map. Also, experts in the history of Real Tennis are not aware of a court at Chiswick House.

The annual reports of the Commissioners paint a picture of a well run mental establishment. In 1896 they state 'the rooms are warm and comfortable....' and in 1905: 'We can report in generally favourable terms on the personal condition and dress of the patients' and 'the house continues to be maintained in very good order'. In 1928 when the Commissioners visited on a dull and chilly November day, they commented that 'the open fires burning in so many rooms are very welcome'.

Fig 53. The stable block/service building as it appeared in 1900 (Chiswick House and Gardens Trust)

Dr Thomas Seymour Tuke died in 1917 and his brother ran the asylum alone for the next eight years. According to an article in *Country Life* Dr Tuke fully appreciated the value and excellence of Chiswick House with its long architectural and social history, 'but, though he does his utmost to maintain uninjured both the fabric and the grounds, it can naturally no longer be kept up as in the ducal days, and it suffers from the removal of so much that made it a very museum of art objects...'[25] There were some casualties, though, a large looking glass was broken by an 'obstreperous patient', also a statue of Apollo 'with which a patient had had a difference'.

Dr Tuke did 'with the most laudable zeal' clear away the ivy which was damaging the Classic Bridge, but he had problems with the trees. By 1908 some were in a dangerous state, particularly the very large elms close to the Bowling Green, two of which had fallen, also a cedar tree too close to the house, a branch of which projected onto the portico and was blackening the stonework. As he was not allowed to fell trees without special permission he had to contact the Duke's agent to ask for the Duke's woodman to see what could be done. In 1916 seventeen trees in the grounds were brought down by a great gale, including the finest cedars in front of the house.

---

25   H Avray Tipping 'Chiswick House, Middlesex II' *Country Life*, 16th February 1918, 165

There were problems too with water from the Lake. In 1921 Duke's Ditch (see p57) was silting up and the decision was made to culvert it. A penstock valve was installed to allow water to flow into the lake each day at high tide. With the growth of Chiswick's population the Council was also having a few headaches with surface water drainage and in 1923 put in an outfall sewer from Chesterfield Road to Burlington Lane, through the Lake. Dr Tuke complained that mud removed from the Lake was being dumped in the shrubberies and tried to claim compensation for the nuisance of the sewer construction but the Council would not admit the claim.

When Charles Molesworth Tuke died in 1925, his obituarist wrote that `he worked to make the atmosphere of Chiswick House that of a private country house, and to disassociate it from all appearances of an institution.' The obituary also tells us that: `for some years Chiswick House has been the centre of local social life and its grounds the venue of many a function designed to assist deserving causes, or to add to the brightness of life'.[26] Tuke's death, combined with the 9th Duke of Devonshire's desire to sell the estate, precipitated the end of the Chiswick asylum. It closed in 1928 and most of the patients were transferred to two houses in Pinner.

---

26 *Chiswick Times*, 30th January, 1925,5

Chapter 7

COUNCIL CONTROL (1929-1948)

Death duties had been introduced by the time the 8th Duke died in 1908 and these, combined with the already rather shaky Cavendish family finances, led to the 9th Duke divesting himself of various heirlooms from Chatsworth and some parcels of land. Chiswick House was sold in 1929 to the Middlesex County Council which leased it for 999 years to Brentford and Chiswick Urban District Council. In a speech made by the 10th Duke of Devonshire in 1947 he claimed that his father had sold the Chiswick House estate 'for not much more than half of what could have been obtained on the open market in order that it might be preserved as a heritage for the people of West London'.[1]

As early as 1904 the *Chiswick Times*, reporting a cricket match in the grounds of Chiswick House which the public had been allowed to attend, said wistfully how much Chiswick residents 'must have wished that the place might one day become a public park'. Dr Tuke had been given the option to purchase Chiswick House once his lease ran out and the local paper went on to suggest that the Council should obtain that option from Dr Tuke 'so that the historic mansion and grounds could become a place of recreation for Chiswick people'. [2]

In 1914 with building going up all over Chiswick there were fears that Chiswick House and grounds would also succumb to bricks and mortar. The local paper wrote:

> There is no imminent danger of the property passing into the hands of the builder but the Chiswick Council would be glad if steps could be taken to prevent such a possibility. Its purchase is too great a task for so small a district as Chiswick to undertake. When the time comes for action an appeal will probably be made to the County Councils of London and Middlesex, to the Livery Companies, and probably also to the general public'.[3]

However, the Council did nearly succeed in obtaining Chiswick House in 1926 when it was offered to the Council by the London and Home Counties Electricity Authority which had negotiated its purchase from the Duke of Devonshire. The quid pro quo was that the Council would allocate the Authority 45 acres of land in Duke's Meadows (which the Council had purchased in 1923) on which to build a large electricity generating station, similar to the power station at Battersea.

---

1   *The Journal of the London Society*, issue 294, 1947, 43
2   *Chiswick Times*, 27 May 1904, 4
3   *Chiswick Times*, 13 February 1914, 5

The Council was keen to proceed, but, predictably, the idea was not popular with Chiswick people who formed the Chiswick Electric Works Protest Association. There was also opposition from Barnes Urban District Council, which felt a power station would spoil the view of Chiswick Reach from the Surrey side. The plan was also opposed by the rowing fraternity worried about rowing activities being impeded by the increased number of barges taking coal to and from the power station. A private parliamentary bill in 1927 failed to pass the Parliamentary Examiners and luckily by this date the Central Electricity Generating Board had modified its plans for electricity supply to south east England, declaring that requirements could be met by Fulham and other generating stations.

Two years later, though, in July 1928, the *Brentford & Chiswick Times* was able to trumpet: `Chiswick House Saved: We have the pleasurable announcement to make this morning that Chiswick House and Gardens will be saved from anything like redevelopment for building purposes'.[4] The actual conveyance of the property from the Duke of Devonshire was signed on 24th January 1929.

Fig 54. The Inigo Jones Gateway in 1929, showing a section of the stable block/service buiding on the right and the entrance to the Princes' Garden (Chiswick House and Gardens Trust)

4   *Brentford & Chiswick Times*, 27 July 1928, 7

Although Middlesex County Council put up the bulk of the £81,000 asking price, many other organisations and individuals contributed. This is the full list:

H M the King £50
Middlesex County Council £60,750
London County Council £5,000
Brentford & Chiswick UDC £5,000.
Hammersmith Borough Council £2,500
The Poulter Trust £2,500
London and Greater London Playing Fields Association £1,000
Mr T Wall £1,000
London Parochial Charities £1,000
Kensington Borough Council £1,000
Lt Col W Grant Morden £500
Chiswick Polish Company £500
Smaller sums locally £120
Metropolitan Public Garden Association £50
Chiswick Civic Association £30 [5]

Fig 55. The opening of the grounds of Chiswick House to the public in 1929
(Local Studies, Chiswick Library)

5   *Brentford & Chiswick Times,* 5 October 1928, 4

Gardens open to the public

In April 1929 there was an extensive sale of the furniture and contents in the house and outbuildings which had belonged to the Tukes' asylum, and on July 5 1929 the gardens were opened to the public – `Chiswick House for the People' was the headline in the local paper that day.[6] The opening ceremony was performed by HRH Prince George (later the Duke of Kent) who arrived in a motorcade and proceeded to the front of Chiswick House along a route lined by Girl Guides and Boy Scouts. His formal declaration that the park was to be `a public space and recreation ground for all time' was followed by a dedicatory prayer from the Reverend Eric Hamilton, Vicar of Chiswick. The Prince then made a brief tour of the house and grounds, paying particular attention to the Princes' Garden (see p72) which was still maintained. The chairman of the Brentford and Chiswick Urban District Council, Councillor Cressy, planted a Douglas fir in the Grand Avenue to commemorate the opening of the garden.

The first act of vandalism, the scourge of public parks, occurred in October 1930 when the local paper reported a `night of outrage' in the grounds of Chiswick House. Vandals had daubed the statues with red, green, blue and dark brown paint and covered them with graffiti.[7]

What the Council did

The minutes of the Parks and Open Spaces Committee of Brentford and Chiswick Council [8] provide a guide as to how the Council looked after its new, illustrious acquisition. One of the Committee's first suggestions was to consider renaming Chiswick House. The local paper called this a `monstrous suggestion' and it was dropped.

In 1931 it was decided to open the `Mansion House' for inspection by the public, initially, only on Sundays between 12 and 4pm but, by 1932, on Thursdays and Saturdays as well. Various organisations, such as the Brentford & Chiswick Local History Society, the London Society, the London and Middlesex Archaeological Society and the Charles Lamb Society were given permission to make private tours of the house. Artist Joseph William Topham Vinall was allowed to exhibit his pictures in the house, but these were required to be removed when the Chiswick Group of Artists mounted their own exhibition in 1936.

Now the grounds had become a public park, additional entrances were needed. These were made in Staveley Road (1931), on the Great Chertsey Road (A316) and in Park Road. The Staveley Road entrance was initially only opened when cricket matches were taking place, but, in 1932, the Council decided to open it each day. The iron gates at Staveley Road were originally one of the several gates to Brentford's famous fruit and vegetable market which was along the stretch of Chiswick High

6   *Brentford & Chiswick Times*, 5 July 1929, 7

7   *Brentford & Chiswick Times*, 30 October 1930, 5

8   Brentford and Chiswick Urban District Council: Minutes of the Parks and Open Spaces Committee (Local Studies, Chiswick Library)

Fig 56. Gates to Brentford Market. One of these gates is now at the Staveley Road entrance to Chiswick House (Local Studies, Chiswick Library)

Road from Chiswick Roundabout to Kew Bridge. They were removed when a covered market building was put up in 1906.

In 1934 the original entrance to Chiswick House on the A316, which had been walled up by the 6th Duke, was re-opened with a pair of new gates bought by the Council. They had originally been the gates of the demolished Grosvenor House, Park Lane. They had been designed by Henry Clutton and erected in Park Lane in 1881. At Park Road a timber-boarded gate with brick piers was installed.

In the early 1930s public conveniences were built near the cricket field and by the Duke's Avenue entrance, a 'Children's Corner' was made in a triangular piece of land adjoining Duke's Avenue, and a drinking fountain was erected in 1934 with money bequeathed by the late Mr Hopkin Morris.[9]

The Council felt that sports facilities were important in a public park and built hard tennis courts (completed 1932) and a hockey field. Plans for a miniature golf course were shelved in favour of two putting greens. Permission was given to Chiswick Cricket Club, Turnham Green Cricket Club and St Georges Medical Hospital Cricket Club to use the existing cricket pitch.

The Council also saw the need to provide refreshments and in 1932 a café was opened in ground floor rooms in the east wing of the house. From 1934 the café, and a kiosk by the cricket pitch, were run by Messrs Greeves Bros. They were also licensed to provide deckchairs in the grounds.

---

9   He was the man responsible for renovating the almshouses at Strand-on-the-Green

Another early Council decision was the demolition of the outbuildings which were in a poor state of repair. The proposal to demolish the stable block/service building (Grosvenor Wing), which had after all been built in the 17th century, resulted in a letter from the Duke of Devonshire's solicitors complaining that the Duke had not been asked for his consent which was required under the covenant with the Middlesex County Council. There was also a protest from the Society for the Protection of Ancient Buildings which suggested that the building should be used instead for housing council workers.

However, the Duke granted a licence and the stable block and most of the other outbuildings were demolished in 1933 (this also included all but the eastern section of South Lodge). The Council planned to grass over the cleared area, and create a small rose garden.

The Conservatory was collapsing. The Council accepted the tender of £2,188 from Messenger and Company of Loughborough to substantially rebuild the Conservatory in 1933. The superstructure was completely remodelled and the original glass framework replaced with a patent clear span bowstring steel and timber rafter structure.

One of the Committee's tasks was to approve and issue permits to people and organisations wishing to use the house and grounds. Individuals were given permission to sketch, paint or take photos in the grounds; organisations such as the West London Hospital and the RSPCA to hold fêtes and an annual Dogs Jamboree; the local church to hold open air services on Sunday evenings in the summer months; brownies to hold a picnic in `the Dell'; the Chiswick Philanthropic Society to give tea and an entertainment to the Old Folks of Chiswick; scouts to hold their annual sports day, and band performances to take place on summer Sunday evenings.

Refused were applications for horse riding in the park; a proposal to relocate the bandstand in Duke's Meadows to Chiswick House grounds; the setting up of a bird sanctuary (the Council was sympathetic but would not finance it) and in 1937 a Mr P Horncastle was refused permission to shoot rats in the park. Instead, the Council called in Middlesex County Council's official rat catcher with the result that a large number were destroyed. Rats were not the only problem; mosquitoes were rampant in 1936 apparently due to the fact that the stakes embedded in the margins of the Lake were so close together that the fish could not get behind them to eat the mosquito larvae.

The Gatehouse was a bit of an anomaly in a publicly-owned park since it was the private freehold property of Dr Charles Molesworth Tuke's widow who lived there with her three daughters. Middlesex County Council was seeking to purchase it from 1932. The relationship with Mrs Tuke seems to have been an uneasy one. She was apparently wrongly occupying three strips of land belonging to the Council. Negotiations over this had gone on for a number of years and eventually legal action was threatened. However, in 1937 Mrs Tuke agreed to sell the Gatehouse to Middlesex County Council for £5,000, the sale to take place three months after her death, but before 1956 at the latest. Mrs Tuke was allowed to continue occupying the three strips of land, but was required to pay 1/- a year rental for them. She died in 1940.

The Committee, wanting to publicise Chiswick House to attract more visitors suggested to London Transport that a poster be produced. This (see Fig 57) was issued in 1937, and there were others in 1962 and 1964.

In 1935 part of the ceiling in one of the rooms in the house fell down, the roof leaked and there were dry rot spores `as big as footballs'. The deteriorating condition of the house and grounds was the subject of a letter to the Council from the Private Secretary to HM Queen Mary in 1937.[10]   The Committee minutes report huffily: `We feel that if Her Majesty had been aware of certain facts and circumstances her observations concerning the condition of the grounds would not have been made'.

Nevertheless, the Queen's letter resulted in HM Office of Works undertaking a survey of the house without charge to the Council. This report, combined with a report from the Forest Products Research Laboratory on 'the dry rot prevalent in the building's woodwork', revealed that Chiswick House required extensive structural repairs and redecoration - at considerable cost. Work to repair the roof began in 1939 and continued until 1941 but further work had to be suspended for the duration of the War.

The War Years

Thankfully, no bombs dropped on Chiswick House itself but there were 15 `incidents' in the gardens.[11] The worst of these occurred during the Blitz in September and October 1940, when high explosive bombs damaged the Conservatory and fell on the north side of the Lake between the Ionic Temple and the Classic Bridge. On 23rd February 1944 a high explosive bomb broke the surface water drain running through the

Fig 57. Chiswick House by Vera Ross, 1937 (© TfL from the London Transport Museum Collection)

centre of the Lake, with the result that the Lake drained itself and, although refilled, still had defects in March 1945. The V2 rocket which exploded in Staveley Road in September 1944 caused further damage in the grounds.

---

10 Queen Mary had known Chiswick House since her youth when she came to visit her cousins, the children of the Prince of Wales. In her latter years she was in the habit of visiting Chiswick every spring to see the camellias in the Conservatory followed by the cherry trees in Staveley Road. A wreath, made from the Chiswick House camellias was sent to St George's Chapel, Windsor for her funeral in 1953.

11 *Record of Incidents Caused by Enemy Action* (the Bomb book Local Studies, Chiswick Library)

At the beginning of the war the ARP (Air Raid Precautions) had a storage depot at Chiswick House which it also used for training volunteers, but it was decided that Chiswick House was too inaccessible and the depot was moved to the Army and Navy depository in Chiswick High Road. Trenches were dug for an air raid shelter which could accommodate 170 (this was probably near the Corney Road gate); an auxiliary fire station for the National Fire Service used some rooms in the house and the Home Guard had an ammunition store in the grounds with a field kitchen in the Deer House. Allotments were made in the Hockey Field and the garden of the Gatehouse by the Duke's Avenue entrance. The Council set aside three quarters of an acre to produce food which was also cultivated in the greenhouses (tomatoes particularly). Rabbits were bred in the old Fives Court (see p79) and pigs were kept by the Chiswick Allotments Pig Club in an old carpenter's shop. Fishing was allowed in the lake at a charge of 2s a day (free for pensioners).

The gardens were open to the public throughout the war with refreshments and deckchairs available from Greeves Brothers. Sporting activities carried on and in November 1941 the Council passed a resolution allowing games to be played on Sundays from 10.30am instead of the previous 2.30pm. The tennis courts continued to be used and in 1946 a rounders pitch was made for use by the nearby Chiswick School for Girls. A charity boxing tournament was held in aid of the Brentford and Chiswick War Appeals Committee in 1943.

Fig 58. The overgrown Orange Tree Garden in about 1929 (Chiswick House and Gardens Trust)

Standing   J. Franklin, D. Tregear, I. Axworthy, G. Heape, R. Routledge, G. Marsh, H. Sharp, I. Gray, S. M. Brown, J. Warr, A. C. Rose, H. Ventham
J. R. Robertson, F. Johnson, F. Gillett
Seated   I. Compton, H. Coombe, A. Thompson, S. Sibley, I. S. Pickering, J. D. Robertson, The Mayor of Brentford and Chiswick, D. Compton,
R. S. Aldington, W. J. Edrich, D. Marchant, Capt. Milner, F. Hazell
MIDDLESEX COUNTY v TURNHAM GREEN   August 7th, 1949

Fig 59. Cricket match at Chiswick House between Middlesex County CC and Turnham Green & District, 1949. Denis Compton is sitting 6th from the right; Bill Edrich, 4th from the right (Courtesy of Wyn Coombe and Jim Lawes)

Cricket is the sport that crops up most in the minutes of the Parks and Open Spaces Committee and by the end of the war the pitch was in great demand, presumably due to a shortage of cricket pitches with grounds turned over to war-time uses. It was just after the war that cricket began to be played in earnest at Chiswick House. In 1946 the Turnham Green Cricket Club (president the Duke of Devonshire) was given permission by the Council to play on the cricket pitch at weekends. There was no pavilion in those days; the changing rooms were two small huts and tea was taken in a marquee erected each week. For several years celebrity cricket matches were organised every summer, often to raise money for the Middlesex County Cricket Club. Crowds, running into thousands, came to see the likes of Dennis Compton, Bill Edrich, the Bedser twins, Tony Lock, Colin Cowdrey and local hero Patsy Hendren.

Fig 60. The Deer House in 1947 (Reproduced by permission of English Heritage, NMR)

Fig 61. The Deer House, 2011 (© Adam Watson)

Since most people were not able to leave home for summer holidays during the war, the Government encouraged councils to lay on summer entertainments and many of the local entertainments were held at Chiswick House. Dances were the most popular events, particularly dancing on the grass and concerts were well attended. There were beauty pageants on Bank Holidays `though the beauties were, perhaps, somewhat bashful'; also talent contests, `though the talents were a little lacking'.

In 1944 a record crowd attended the Pony Parade and Sports.

After the war, the Council's Community Feeding and Catering Committee decided to take over responsibility for running the café and providing deck chairs and, in 1948, the contract with Messrs Greeves Bros was terminated.

So this was Chiswick House at the end of the war, battered, but still intact. Although the house itself had not been hit, the bombardment meant

Fig 62. The lioness in the Exedra. It was probably sculpted by Peter Scheemakers (© Margaret Drury)

that almost all its windows were broken. In the garden, the avenues were overgrown; ivy rampaged over the garden buildings; statues were toppling over and hidden by undergrowth; bamboo colonised the Orange Tree Garden and its `sedgy pool' was half choked with weeds and rushes. `A shabby, decadent kind of beauty – an atmosphere of vanished magnificence and taste' is how Frank Clark, author of *The English Landscape Garden* (1948), described Chiswick in his 1941 diary.

Chapter 8

HOUSE GIVEN TO THE NATION (1948-1982)

With the war over, the Georgian Group[1] took up the cudgels about Chiswick House, with a letter to the Municipal Borough of Brentford and Chiswick in June 1946 asking what arrangements the Council proposed for its restoration. The Council replied that because of the volume of war-damage repairs and the need for labour and materials required to solve the heavy post-war housing problem `some difficulty would be met in diverting labour to restore this building'.[2]

The Georgian Group wrote again in November of the same year saying that:

> The Group, while cognisant of the natural pride which the council takes in the building and their good intentions in the matter of repair, feel strongly that Chiswick House is too important a building to remain the responsibility of a single local authority, which already has extensive and urgent commitments in other directions, and suggest that the burden of restoring and maintaining it in a proper state of repair should be laid on broader shoulders; moreover that it is obviously desirable that the building should be put to some appropriate use, in view of the number of bodies which are interested in the future of the building, and the somewhat complex situation which arises owing to the fact that the building is owned by one local authority and leased by another, it has been suggested that the most useful first step would be a conference of representatives of all interested parties.[3]

The conference was held on 10 June 1947 and attended by representatives of the Middlesex County Council, the Borough of Brentford and Chiswick, the Georgian Group, the National Trust and the London Society. Representatives were in favour of the proposal for the restoration and maintenance of Chiswick House on a national basis. This was followed in August 1947 by an informal meeting at the House of Commons in which local people and representatives from the National Trust, the Museums Society and the Georgian Group were invited to give their views on the future of Chiswick House. There was great enthusiasm for preserving the property and for using it as a cultural centre for the Borough of Brentford and Chiswick.

In 1947 Claud Phillimore (later 4th Baron Phillimore), a founder member of the Georgian Group and a neo-Georgian architect who ran his own architectural practice, was sufficiently concerned about the state of Chiswick House, which he described as `battered by bombs and corroded by dry rot and disuse', to draw up a plan for its

---

1   This had been founded in 1937 with the aim of protecting and preserving Georgian buildings, monuments and landscapes.

2   Brentford & Chiswick Council: Minutes of the Parks and Open Spaces Committee 11th June 1946

3   *Ibid* 27th November 1946

restoration. He followed this up with an article in *Country Life*. Phillimore proposed that the wings should be demolished; that the gardens should be restored; that furniture, statuary, pictures, books etc should be acquired so that 'the Villa may be arranged, as nearly as may be, as it was in Lord Burlington's time'. He also proposed the formation of a body of Trustees and of a Friends of Chiswick House.[4]

Phillimore's plan led to more discussions between the interested parties and the local council accepted the proposal that 'Chiswick House including certain temples, buildings and ornaments in the grounds' be taken over by the Ministry of Works – with the proviso that the Council continue to 'use a portion of the house as a café.'[5]

The house was presented to the nation under Section 2 of the Ancient Monument Consolidation and Amendment Act 1913 in August 1948. The legal deed of gift document, though, was not drawn up until 19th April 1956, which explains the date on the inscription in the stonework of the house. This commemorative plaque, which had been under discussion by the Council since 1948, reads:

> Erected 1725-30 by the Third Earl of Burlington. Acquired 1929 from the ninth duke of Devonshire by Middlesex County Council with contributions from HM King George V, the former Urban District Council of Brentford & Chiswick & others. Given 1956 by the County and Borough Councils to the Ministry of Works by whom it was repaired and opened to the public 1958.

The gift included twenty two of the structures in the garden, but not the Conservatory, the urns, or most of the statues (see Appendix III for more details).

The grounds themselves also remained in the care of the Council. With hindsight this is a shame since local councils neither have the funding nor the management expertise to maintain historic gardens, such as Chiswick House, as anything other than public parks, of which the Council had several.

In 1949 the Architectural Council of the Festival of Britain 1951 (Chairman Hugh Casson) planned for Chiswick House to be one of the venues for the Festival. Functions proposed to be held at Chiswick were a Masque called 'Lord Burlington and Mr Kent' with music by Handel; a performance of Midsummer Night's Dream; a costume ball'; a festival of folk dancing; a Chiswick Pageant and a music festival. There were to be firework displays and illuminations in the grounds. The idea of using Chiswick for the Festival was supported by the Georgian Group which was confident that Chiswick would prove as popular as Vauxhall Gardens or Ranelagh were in former times. The Architectural Council pressed the Ministry of Works for the complete restoration of Chiswick House in time for the Festival, but the Ministry was unable to comply and the proposed events never took place.[6]

4   Claud Phillimore 'A Plan for Chiswick House', *Country Life*, July 18th 1948, 126-7
5   Minutes of the Parks and Open Spaces Committee 11th October 1948
6   National Archives Ministry of Works file 25/46, 1949

Fig 63. The steps at the back of the house which were removed by the 6th Duke of Devonshire but reconstructed in the 1950s (© Adam Watson)

The Architectural Council also endorsed the Georgian Group's suggestion that the `Warren Gates' should be re-sited at Chiswick House to make a more impressive entrance for visitors. These are the gates (made by a Mr Warren in the early 18th century) now at the Piccadilly entrance to Green Park (see p56).[7] However, the Ministry of Works restored the gates to Green Park, saying that it was not possible to comply with the request since the gates had been bought for the nation by public subscription.

House reconstructed

Removal of the wings of Chiswick House was, and remains, a very contentious issue. Phillimore's reasoning for their demolition was this:

> Burlington's villa is a building of unique natural importance whereas the building as it stands is a hotchpotch, with a certain amount of charm, but no great architectural merit and the very large sums of money necessary to put the whole in a state of repair would not be worth the expense.

The Georgian Group also thought demolition of the wings would not be a loss. The decision was criticised, though, by architectural historian, Nikolaus Pevsner. In a lecture he gave in 1952 he complained that such actions as removing wings were being carried out indiscriminately to `restore purity'; but he thought the time would come

7   *Ibid*

when people looked at pictures of these buildings as they formerly were, and said
'what a pity'.[8]

The Ministry of Works' restoration plan was drawn up in 1951 and work began
under the supervision of Patrick A Faulkner ARIBA with G H Chettle the principal
historic adviser. They worked from original designs, old drawings, Burlington's
letters, inventories made for the Dukes of Devonshire and material discovered during
the reconstruction.

The wings were removed and the walls of the villa behind the wings reconstructed.
Woodworm and dry rot were eradicated. The later casement windows were replaced
with 18th-century sashes and the original obelisk-shaped chimneys rebuilt. The
outside stairs on the garden front were re-instated using original moulded stone
fragments which had been re-used when the wings were built.

*Fig 64. When Tom Greeves drew this sketch in 1958 the wings had just been demolished but the Link
Building not yet re-instated. So this is how Chiswick House would have appeared in 1729*
(© Eleanor Greeves)

Inside the house, the floors of coloured concrete were taken up and stone floors
put down; discoloured gilding was refreshed and the light brown coating which
had been painted over the ceiling in the Blue Velvet Room, the woodwork in the Bed
Chamber and on all the internal doors was removed. Research in the Chatsworth
Archive established the original colour schemes of the rooms, and green, red and blue

flock wallpapers were made up using contemporary patterns from the Victoria and Albert Museum. The work cost £130,000 – a great deal more than the initial estimate of £20,000.

The house was opened to the public on 24th July 1958 when it was officially handed over to the Ministry of Works. The Minister of Works, the Rt Hon Hugh Molson, received the formal deed of the transfer of ownership of the house from the two local authorities.

Fig 65. *The Gallery in Chiswick House*
(© Adam Watson)

A distinguished company attended the opening. It included dignitaries from the Middlesex County Council, Brentford and Chiswick Council, the Ministry of Works, Lady Dorothy Macmillan, wife of the Prime Minister, the 11th Duke of Devonshire and members of his family. The Duke began his opening speech by saying: `Chiswick is restored to all its glory and how glorious it is'. He went on to give a brief history of the house and to praise the Ministry and its staff for their skilled restoration. He concluded by recalling his earliest recollection of Chiswick as being brought down to watch the boat races from the adjacent Duke's Meadows: ` and how much I wish they were still really my meadows' he said.[9]

Once the scaffolding had been removed from the villa, the Link building, which had been enveloped by one of the wings, was exposed and was reconstructed (completed 1964). Some say its reconstruction was a mistake if the idea was to re-create Burlington's original plan. The Link Building had been added to the villa to join it to the living accommodation in the now non-existent Jacobean house. The Link Building, together with the Summer Parlour, now stands in splendid isolation `linking' nothing with nothing.

Was Chiswick House haunted? A book[10] published in 1974 about haunted Britain claimed that Chiswick House was haunted by a ghostly smell of eggs and bacon. This information apparently given to the book's author by the Custodian of Chiswick House who said that workmen repairing the house had noticed the smell in the wing of the house which had been close to the kitchens.

---

9 *Brentford and Chiswick Times*, 1st August 1958, 5
10 Andrew Green *Our Haunted Kingdom*, 1974

The grounds

Quite a lot of work was done on the gardens following the re-opening of the house; this owed much to the enthusiasm of the Borough of Brentford and Chiswick's then Superintendent of the Parks Department. Overgrown avenues were cleared and yew hedges planted, the grass steps in the Orange Tree Garden were reshaped, the piers were re-erected in the forecourt in 1952 and the terms (see p35) re-installed. In 1953 the path to the Exedra (made by the Marquess of Bute) was suppressed and the avenue down the centre of the garden re-instated with the urns and sphinxes along its length.

Unfortunately some of this enthusiasm seems to have been misplaced. Hedges were planted in places where there had never been hedges. The plan for the forecourt was taken from Rocque's 1736 plan (see Fig 1) which was the wrong scale and the Orange Tree Garden was inaccurately restored.

Fig 66. The modernist café designed by George Chuter in 1952 but demolished in 2009
(© Gill Mobbs, Chiswick House and Gardens Trust)

The Council's café had of course been destroyed when the wings of the house were removed. Refreshments were served from a marquee before a new café was built in the area known as the Princes' Garden. A shortage of Council architectural staff meant that the design of the café was farmed out to a private architect, George Chuter with a practice in Kingston-upon-Thames. His `modernist' café was opened in 1952 with the catering put out to tender again. This café (rather unkindly dismissed as `only one up from a bus shelter' by Clive Aslet in the *Daily Telegraph*)[11] was very popular with local people, but it was rather small and on the line of the Old Burlington Lane which it was planned to reinstate.

---

11 Clive Aslet *Pleasure Gardens*, Daily Telegraph, 3rd November 2007, 71

Fig 67. The cricket pavilion which was erected in 1956 (Chiswick House and Gardens Trust)

The Cricket Pavilion was built in 1956 at a cost of £7,000. Designed by G H Harrison, ARIBA, it apparently caused 'quite a stir among builders and architects throughout the country', according to the local paper. *The Builder* magazine devoted four pages of photographs and designs describing it.[12] In the mid 1950s the Old Meadonians Cricket Club (the old boys of Chiswick School) shared the pitch with Turnham Green Cricket Club.

Peacocks were re-introduced to the gardens in 1957. A peacock and peahen were brought from London Zoo and initially roamed around freely. However, unmerciful teasing from local youths meant that it became necessary to pen them behind the Conservatory. In 1961, after they had failed to incubate any eggs, three eggs were placed under a broody hen in St Mary's Convent on the opposite side of Burlington Lane. Two were hatched and the baby birds (with mother hen) returned to Chiswick House. But the peacocks pecked their offspring to death and in the end the peacock and peahen were taken to Kew Gardens.

In 1958 the western avenue of the Patte d'oie, formerly leading to the Bagnio (see p21) was cut through to the Classic Bridge (see p45). The attempt to restore the paths in the Patte d'oie came in for criticism since the Bagnio and the Domed Building (see p21) to which the avenues formerly led had both been demolished in the 18th century. In 1970 the Ministry of Public Buildings and Works (the renamed Ministry of Works) erected a window from one of the demolished wings of the house as an 'eyecatcher' in the central avenue. The Classic Bridge was repaired in 1970 and the grand avenue leading from the house to the Patte d'oie restored in 1971 with a £600 grant from the Leche Trust.

In the late 1950s a strip of land was shaved off the grounds of Chiswick House for the construction of the Cromwell Road extension (A4) linking Kensington to the Great West Road. This road, which effectively sliced Chiswick in half, had been planned for 40 years. The Duke's Avenue entrance was moved back 74 ft and new boundary walls, gates and gate piers with new sphinxes erected in the early 1960s. The truncation of the grounds meant that the Children's Playground was lost as was the keeper's North Lodge (a new bungalow with the same name was put up in 1960).

In 1965, after the reorganisation of local government, Chiswick was incorporated into the London Borough of Hounslow and work on the gardens lost impetus. Reports

---

12 *Brentford & Chiswick Times*, 28th December 1956, 4

in the local papers suggest that the 1960s and 1970s were rather bleak periods for Chiswick House. Visitors to the house fell from 27,000 in 1959 to 20,600 by 1971. In the gardens the ducks on the lake were dying in 1969 – killed by leeches. A sad event occurred in 1967 when a troubled 17 year-old girl hanged herself in the Ionic Temple, and in 1969 the statuette of a skipping girl was stolen from the Conservatory. The statuette, sculpted by Mary Thornycroft (mother of shipbuilder, John Isaac) had been bought by the Council from Dr Tuke.[13]

Kids on bikes were intimidating visitors, motorcycles were roaring round the grounds and lead was stolen from the roofs of the Ionic Temple and Link Building. In 1978, 12 birds, mainly geese, were found with their heads cut off, and dogs were being killed by Paraquat poisoning. There were several incidents of vandalism and hooliganism; in 1979 a gardener was stabbed by a gang of youths (he was not seriously hurt), `just one of the muggings that have plagued visitors to Chiswick House during the last year', reported a local paper.[14]

Fig 68. The Eyecatcher, put up in 1970 in the avenue which originally led to the Domed Building. The Eyecatcher is one of the windows from a demolished wing of the house (© Margaret Drury)

On a brighter note, the Council made some money by allowing filming in the grounds. In 1966 the Beatles filmed promotional material for their songs `Paperback Writer' and `Rain' here (Mick Jagger was photographed inside the house for Vanity Fair in 1991).

In 1977 the Queen celebrated her Silver Jubilee. Chiswick House commemorated the event with a two week festival in June. Events included an `Evening with Lord Burlington', Gilbert and Sullivan favourites, a jazz concert, a classical concert, folk and rock music, a performance of Midsummer Night's Dream, children's plays, poetry and prose readings, and 19th-century Variety and Music Hall, ending with fireworks. Chiswick House gardener, Harry Barber, who lived with his family in Kent House, was awarded the Queen's Silver Jubilee Medal in recognition of his 50 years continuous service. He had started work in the nursery garden in 1946 as `pot boy'

---

13 It was one of three statues that stood in the Conservatory. Another statue of a `nymph preparing for her bath' is now in Chiswick House near the Summer Parlour; the third, of a young male thought to be Ishmael in the Wilderness, was discovered broken in the Walled Gardens in 2009 but has been restored and placed back in the Conservatory.

14 *Chiswick and Brentford Gazette*, 17 May 1979, 1

Fig 69. The mosaic floor in the Conservatory and two of the three statues which stood around it
(photo by Vera Collingwood ©, Robert Collingwood)

and risen to Senior Area Foreman. In 1978 the house was floodlit for the first time in 20 years.

The Conservatory was badly in need of repair again by 1976, and even worse, the Department of the Environment (which was now responsible for Chiswick House having absorbed the Ministry of Public Buildings and Works in 1970) threatened to remove the Conservatory from the listed buildings register. It was originally listed Grade I (the highest status) as it was thought to have been designed by Joseph Paxton in the 1830s. However, it had been discovered by chance that it was actually the work of Samuel Ware in 1813.[15] Luckily the threat was withdrawn.

Water supply to the Lake was causing flooding problems and in 1977 the penstock valve (see p81) was replaced by a flap valve which can be opened manually when the water level in the Lake becomes too low so that water can flood in from the Thames.

The demolition of the wings has affected how Chiswick House can be used today and was probably why in the mid 1970s the Department of the Environment proposed to erect a huge single storey annexe, the same size as the house and enclosing the Summer Parlour on three sides. This building was to function as a facility for the

15 A Chiswick resident's letter to *The Times*, complaining about the state of the Conservatory, resulted in an architect in Birmingham sending a specification for its design from the office of Samuel Ware which he had discovered in a notebook of one of Ware's pupils. 'The Paxton Conservatory' *Brentford & Chiswick Local History Society Journal* 2, 1984, 27

warders, a place for refreshment, a large Interpretation Centre and somewhere for holding entertainments. The proposal generated heated controversy. The Georgian Group, supported by the Society for the Protection of Ancient Buildings, objected strongly, and the proposal was withdrawn in 1978.

Fig 70. Plan of the Department of the Environment's proposed extension to Chiswick House which would have functioned as an interpretation centre and facility for wardens. The plan provoked heated controversy and was dropped (Chiswick House and Gardens Trust)

In 1980 the Gatehouse was let out as offices. It had been used as a Youth Centre between 1946 and 1950, then by Chiswick Polytechnic for adult education classes and as the local centre for Civil Defence. Empty from 1977 it had suffered a severe fire in 1979 but had been renovated.

In 1999 the Gatehouse was sold to a film production company and in 2005/6 it was converted into flats.

Chapter 9

CONSERVATION
AND RESTORATION (1982-2011)

By the 1980s the state of the house and gardens was again causing concern and it was agreed that a fresh initiative was needed. In 1982 the Directorate of Ancient Monuments and Historic Buildings department of the Department of the Environment (which was now responsible for Chiswick House) and the London Borough of Hounslow established a working party to address the knotty question of how to balance what was both a public amenity and a heritage site of national importance. The working party commissioned a thorough historical survey from landscape architects Travers Morgan Planning and held a public consultation.

Fig 71. Lead sphinx designed by John Cheere, once in the gardens but taken inside the house in 1994 (© Adam Watson)

In 1984 the exterior of Chiswick House was painted green, `Chiswick Green' as the locals dubbed it. The Council had carried out this work on its own initiative, without the knowledge of the Department of the Environment. By 1986 Chiswick House had become the responsibility of English Heritage[1], a body set up under the National Heritage Act 1983 to take over the function for maintaining England's historic buildings from the Department of the Environment.

The grounds had to be closed for four weeks following the hurricane of October 1987 when several trees came down, others lost limbs, one branch damaging the Classic Bridge. Private functions were now allowed at Chiswick House, one in 1987 churned up the grounds badly and residents complained about the noisy fireworks.

---

1   English Heritage was set up in 1984 but only assumed its full powers in 1986 when historic properties were transferred to it from the Directorate of Ancient Monuments and Historic Buildings of the Department of the Environment.

Fig 72. The Cascade which was put back in working order in 1997 (© Adam Watson)

In 1988 English Heritage and London Borough of Hounslow signed a Joint Management Agreement with plans for the restoration and improved maintenance of the gardens over an eight year period.

Work began immediately. The Lake was dredged and an archaeological excavation carried out to determine the position of the cedars in the forecourt. The following year new cedars were planted there. Unfortunately these were the wrong species - Atlantic cedars, rather than the original Cedars of Lebanon. Also in 1989 the Ionic Temple was repaired, new tubs were made for the Orange Tree Garden and South Lodge was extensively renovated by artist Barry Martin and others to be used as his studio.

In 1990 a car park for 50 vehicles was constructed, despite opposition from residents, and repairs were carried out to the Conservatory. In 1991 the rose beds in the Rosary (see p46), which had been grassed over, were planted out again - so successfully that the Rosary won a Highly Commended Ford Conservation Award. The gates at the Great Chertsey Road (A316) entrance were repaired and lime trees were planted in the Grove in 1992. The original trees are thought to have been elms but the high risk of Dutch elm disease determined the choice of limes.

In 1994 yew hedges were planted along the Raised Terrace which was seeded with grass and the avenue to the Classic Bridge was restored. The lead sphinx in the garden, which had deteriorated, was removed to the house and replaced in the garden with a stone copy (this was on its plinth for less than six weeks before vandals beheaded it).

The three Roman statues in the Exedra were also taken inside the house and replaced with copies; likewise the Roman relief on the Burlington Lane obelisk. The Inigo Jones Gateway which had been closed for restoration re-opened in 1995. In 1996, the gates and gate piers to the Walled Gardens were repaired and refurbished, and the avenue leading from the Burlington Gate Obelisk to the Classic Bridge was moved back to its original alignment.

Fig 73. *One of a pair of side tables in the Gallery with tops of Italian marble and gilded wooden bases which were probably designed by William Kent. This table was returned to the house in 1996*
(© Adam Watson)

Perhaps the most exciting restoration of all began in 1996 when the Cascade, which never seems to have operated properly, was put in working order with a grant from the Heritage Lottery Fund. It was re-opened by the present Earl of Burlington in 1997. In that year too the pebbled floor[2] under the old Orangery (Arcade) was surveyed, the path from the Burlington Lane Gate over the Cascade was made, the wildflower meadow planted (it had been tried several years earlier but with limited success) and the looped path to the Oriental Plane tree (see p57) was restored. The original plane tree, which extended nearly 100ft, had gone but a young plane tree was put in its place. In 2002 a new sundial[3] was installed to the south of the Italian Garden to replace the sundial from the Moreton Hall garden which had disappeared in the 1980s.

One of the events that took place in the garden in 1998 was an all-day concert by the Strawbs, given to celebrate the group's 30th anniversary.

Community involvement

Chiswick people love the gardens and various local groups have been formed to safeguard and maintain them. In 1984, the Chiswick House Friends was established. A registered charity, its aims are to conserve, protect, promote and enhance Chiswick House and gardens. It also raises funds for special projects, such as the purchase of

---

2   There are mosaic floors in the Conservatory, the Deer House and on the site of the Orangery/Arcade. The Conservatory floor dates from the time of the 6th Duke of Devonshire but the Orangery and Deer House floors are thought to be contemporary with those buildings
3   The sundial was given by Mrs Linda Bland as a memorial to her son and daughter-in-law

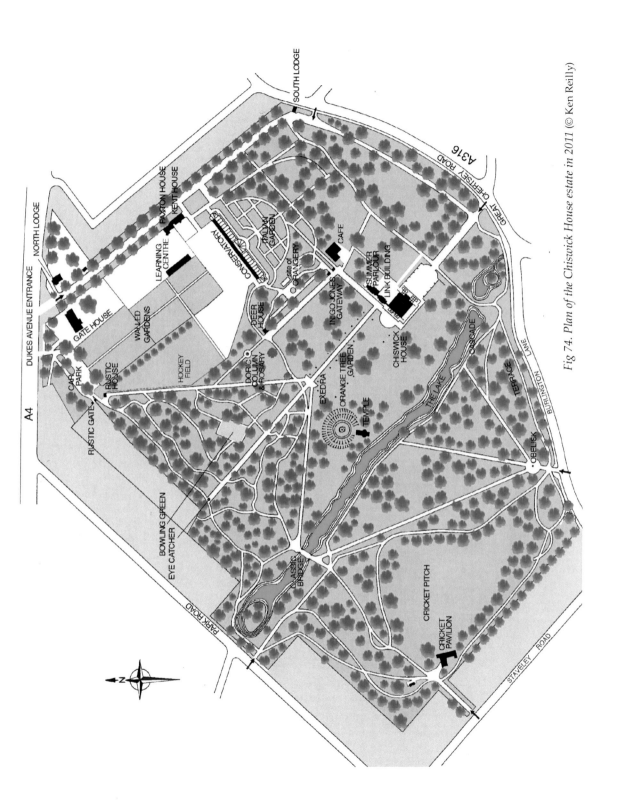

Fig 74. Plan of the Chiswick House estate in 2011 (© Ken Reilly)

105

Fig 75. The Goosefoots, the volunteers who tend the gardens at Chiswick House
(© Nigel Corrie, English Heritage)

furniture, sculpture and paintings to go in the house. Since 2004 the Friends have laid on opera performances in the gardens every summer. Immensely popular, these are almost always sold out. Parkwatch, an independent group created to ensure that the grounds remain a safe and pleasant place, started in 2002 but was replaced by the park wardens in 2010. CHOW (Chiswick House Owners Dog Walkers), a lobbying association representing the interests of those who regularly walk their dogs in the grounds was set up in 2006. CHOW members subscribe to a voluntary code for dog walkers and organise the annual dog show in association with the Chiswick House Friends. In 2003 The Goosefoots were formed. These are local volunteers who give half a day each week to help maintain the gardens.

The Chiswick House Kitchen Garden project began in 2005. The walled gardens belonging to Moreton Hall (see p53) had always been out of bounds to visitors since the park opened to the public in 1929. Hounslow Council used it as a nursery garden to cultivate seeds and saplings for planting out elsewhere in the Borough. It was also let out as a venue for functions organised by local groups, such as the scouts. In 1955, local archery club, `The Duke's Bowmen' was given permission to hold sessions there one night a week. In 1983 the Council, wanting to extend the nursery garden, booted out a beekeeper who had maintained hives in the garden for many years.

Council policy changed in the 1990s and there were various abortive plans for the use of the garden. In 1992 the local paper announced that the garden was to be made over to the Horticultural Training and Co-operative Employment Unit to help people with mental and physical handicaps learn new skills in horticulture and market their produce. In 1996 it was proposed to make it into an AIDS Memorial Garden.

In 2002 the Council planned to turn the Southern Walled Garden into a small-scale commercial nursery business to be called Chiswick House Heritage Plant Centre. This dismayed local resident Karen Liebreich and she persuaded the Council to allow a strip of the garden to be cultivated as a kitchen garden by volunteers (luckily, the retail plan had been vetoed by English Heritage). Local schools were encouraged to bring groups of children each week to help look after the garden and learn about growing plants, each session ending with a salad picnic where the children could sample their own produce. Regular work sessions for adults were introduced and occasional Open Days when people could admire the garden and buy its surplus produce. This local community project was very successful with the kitchen garden winning awards, appearing on television programmes and in the national and local press. In December 2009 the Kitchen Garden Association handed over responsibility for the upkeep of the garden to the Chiswick House and Gardens Trust.

Help from the Heritage Lottery Fund

Cutbacks in funding during the 1990s meant that Hounslow Council felt it was not able to maintain the gardens at Chiswick House from the Council budget, even at the current level. An application was made to the Heritage Lottery Fund in 1997, which was successful. However, due to the departure of the Landscape Architect and difficulties and delays in finding a suitable replacement, the HLF money was not released and it was decided to withdraw that bid and re-apply. A Stage I bid was prepared but, when the Heritage Lottery Fund introduced a new major grant category, the Public Parks Initiative, the HLF suggested that this would be more appropriate – and would provide more funding for the work at Chiswick House. It took some years to prepare, however a £600,000 grant from

Fig 76. Schoolchildren with Karen Liebreich in the Kitchen Garden, 2007, about to picnic on the produce they had helped to grow (© Caroline Ames for the Kitchen Garden Association)

the Wolfson Foundation allowed some advance restoration work to start in 2006. The Burlington Lane Gate and Obelisk were restored, the Camellia Shrubbery was re-planted, an Education facility, now known as the Learing Centre, was created in the Nursery Yard and, most exciting of all, sphinxes were re-instated on the gate piers in the Forecourt. They were cast from the lead sphinx inside the house.

Fig 77. Camellias in bloom at the Camellia Festival, 2011 (© Philip Sarell)

It was becoming increasingly apparent that an integrated approach was needed so that the building and its grounds could be managed and promoted as one single entity.

Thus, in 2005, the charitable Chiswick House and Gardens Trust was formed to oversee the restoration of the gardens and to look after both house and garden under a 99 year lease. The Trust comprises 11 trustees, five appointed by the London Borough of Hounslow (which still contributes towards the upkeep of the grounds); five by English Heritage plus a jointly nominated chairperson.

Since the Phase I lottery bid was made under the Heritage Lottery Fund's Public Parks Initiative, it covered only the gardens, excluding work on the House itself, which may be the subject of a Phase II lottery bid.

The Trust, trying to find a balance between heritage considerations, the importance of the garden as a free-to-enter public park, and the need for financial stability, proposed that the upkeep of the gardens should be largely funded by allowing the house and grounds to be hired out for occasional corporate and private functions. To this end the Trust proposed the erection of a marquee beside the house to be used for functions for about three or four months of the year; a new, larger, restaurant to replace the 1952 café, and the use of the northern part of the Walled Gardens as an overflow car park. These proposals were very controversial both locally and nationally and led to three eminent architectural historians resigning as trustees. They feared that the commercialisation of Chiswick House would demean the site.

In 2008 the Trust learned that the Lottery Bid had been successful and so began a major £12.1m (£7.6m of which came from the Heritage Lottery Fund) restoration project which took nearly two years to complete. Archaeological excavations were carried out in the Walled Gardens to determine the position of the original paths; on the site of the new café where the stable block/service building had originally been; under the concrete platform for the marquee where the Jacobean mansion once stood; by the Rustic Gate to discover the line of Lord Burlington's carriageway; and a dig alongside the ha-ha to reveal the floor of the Orangery/Arcade.

The new café, designed by Caruso St John, was built in 2009 near the Inigo Jones Gateway. It can seat 80 people inside and more outside. The caterer is Company of Cooks which also runs the cafés at Kenwood House and Wisley. To the south of the café a play area for young children was created, in response to the public consultation programme.

The car park was reconfigured to take more cars and the Northern Walled Garden planted out as an Orchard (the Trust decided against designating it as an overflow car park). A new entrance from the car park to the grounds has been

Fig 78. Poster advertising the Chiswick Extravaganza held in the gardens in 1992 (Chiswick House and Gardens Trust)

created by opening up Lord Burlington's old carriage gateway (see p32). A new iron gate has been made for this entrance and another to replace the wooden gate at Park Road. The buildings in the Stable Yard have been renovated for use as staff offices, for educational purposes and for storage.

In the gardens, the garden buildings, statues and urns have been repaired and cleaned. One of the largest projects concerned the Conservatory which was completely rebuilt incorporating the original 19th-century ironwork. The Rosary around the Doric Column has been restored to its 19th- century appearance with roses donated by David Austin Roses. The lion's share of the cost for this was borne by the Chiswick House Friends which also paid for the Portland stone copy of the statue of the Venus de Medici, sculpted by Andrian Melka, which was erected on top of the Doric Column in September 2009 (the original disappeared sometime in the 19th century).

Fig 79. The copy of the Venus de Medici statue, with its sculptor Andrian Melka, erected on the Doric Column in 2009 (© John Armstrong)

Paths around the gardens have been resurfaced, mainly with hoggin (a compact mixture of clay, sand and gravel) and their drainage improved. One new path has been made along what was the original line of Burlington Lane before the 6th Duke arranged to have the line of Burlington Lane changed (see p56). The left hand avenue of the Patte d'oie has been re-aligned to Lord Burlington's original design when it led to his Bagnio (see p21). Hedges have been replanted to their correct proportions and the water supply to the Lake improved. Many trees have been felled, either because they were dead, dangerous, crowding out other trees or spoiling historic views, particularly the view of the lawn. However, new trees have been planted – old varieties of fruit trees in the Orchard, limes in the Grove and eight Cedars of Lebanon in the Forecourt to the house. These were propagated from the existing cedars in the garden. Historic 19th-century varieties of rhododendrons have been propagated and planted in the Serpentine Walk and elsewhere; the layout of the Camellia Shrubbery has been improved and conserved with new planting.

A generous donation from the late Miss Phyllis Bishop has enabled the Italian Garden to be restored to its original design. The yew hedges which enclosed the garden have been removed and replaced with a border consisting of four rows of China roses in front, white lilies with roses trained on rope swags and mophead robinias, about 6ft tall and pruned into shape, behind. The border is backed by camellias and other evergreens.

The Trust now has a team of staff on site including wardens to look after the safety and security of the gardens and an Education Service which encourages schoolchildren to discover the ecological and historical wonders on their doorstep. There are also over 150 volunteers who act as house guides, stewards in the Conservatory, kitchen gardeners and archivists. The annual events programme includes outdoor theatre, concerts, talks, walks and family activities.

In 2011 the Chiswick House and Gardens Trust held the first Chiswick House Camellia Festival. People from all over the world came to view the historic camellia collection and the Festival is now set to become an annual event in the national gardening calendar.

Fig 80. Wassailing in the Southern Walled Garden in 2011. Ribbons are tied to the tree to encourage the new fruit trees to grow (© Hannah Levy)

These, then, are the gardens of Chiswick House in 2011, restored and rejuvenated, for humans and other creatures to enjoy. And there are plenty of `other creatures'. Although the wildlife is perhaps not as exotic as the peacocks (see p98), black swans (see p60) or nightingales `which make sweet music in the evening'[4] mentioned by a visitor in 1904, there are six different species of bats, hedgehogs, foxes, rats and possibly still badgers. There are also myriads of different birds including the raucous but colourful parakeets which love Chiswick House gardens and which have been colonising parks in west London and other parts of the country since about the 1930s.

The restoration of the gardens at Chiswick House was one of two Highly Commended projects in the Landscape Institute Awards of 2010. The gardens also won a Mayor's Safer Parks Award in the top (Gold) category in 2011.

In the same year the Chiswick House café won a Civic Trust Award `for its outstanding contribution to the quality and appearance of the environment'. It was also one of 97 buildings to be given an RIBA award for architectural excellence in 2011. The judges rated it as the best new building in London.

---

4   *Chiswick Times.* 27th May, 1904

APPENDIX I

TIMELINE: OWNERS AND OCCUPIERS OF THE CHISWICK HOUSE ESTATE AND OTHER SIGNIFICANT DATES

1682 Richard Boyle, 1st Earl of Burlington buys Jacobean mansion at Chiswick

1698 Charles Boyle, 2nd Earl of Burlington inherits

1704 Richard Boyle, 3rd Earl of Burlington (1694-1753) inherits

1726-9 Palladian Chiswick House built

1726/7 Three parcels of land added to Chiswick House gardens

1733 3rd Earl of Burlington makes Chiswick his main London home

1753 Death of Richard Boyle. His wife inherits his property in trust

1758 Lady Burlington dies. William Cavendish (1748-1811) who becomes the 5th Duke of Devonshire in 1764 inherits

1788 Jacobean Chiswick House demolished and wings built onto Palladian villa

1811 William George Spencer Cavendish, 6th Duke of Devonshire (1790-1858) inherits

1812 6th Duke purchases Moreton Hall, demolishes the house and adds the land to gardens of Chiswick House

1858 Harriet née Cavendish, Dowager Lady Granville (1785-1862) is left Chiswick House for her lifetime

1862 William Cavendish, 7th Duke of Devonshire (1808-1891) inherits

1863 Chiswick House leased to the Dowager Duchess of Sutherland (1806-1868)

1869 Leased to the Prince of Wales, later Edward VII (until 1877)

1881 Leased to the Marquess of Bute

1891 The 8th Duke of Devonshire (1833-1908) inherits

1892 Leased to the Chiswick House Asylum run by the Tuke brothers

1908 Victor Christian William Cavendish, 9th Duke of Devonshire (1868-1938) inherits

1929 9th Duke of Devonshire sells Chiswick House estate to Middlesex County Council which leases it to Brentford and Chiswick Urban District Council. Gardens are opened to the public

1933 Stable block and other service buildings demolished

1948 Chiswick House (but not the grounds) given to the nation and put under the care of the Ministry of Works which restores the house

1958 Chiswick House opened to the public

1965 Local government re-organisation. Greater London Council take over responsibility for parks from Middlesex County Council which is abolished. The Municipal Borough of Brentford and Chiswick absorbed into the London Borough of Hounslow

1986 English Heritage assumes responsibility for Chiswick House

2005 The Chiswick House and Gardens Trust set up to oversee the garden restoration project and look after both house and gardens thereafter

2008-2010 Garden restoration project carried out

2010 The Chiswick House and Gardens Trust assumes managerial and financial responsibility for the garden and for some of the activities in the house. The Trust is expected to take over day-to-day management of the house within the next few years.

Appendix II Boyle & Cavendish Family Trees

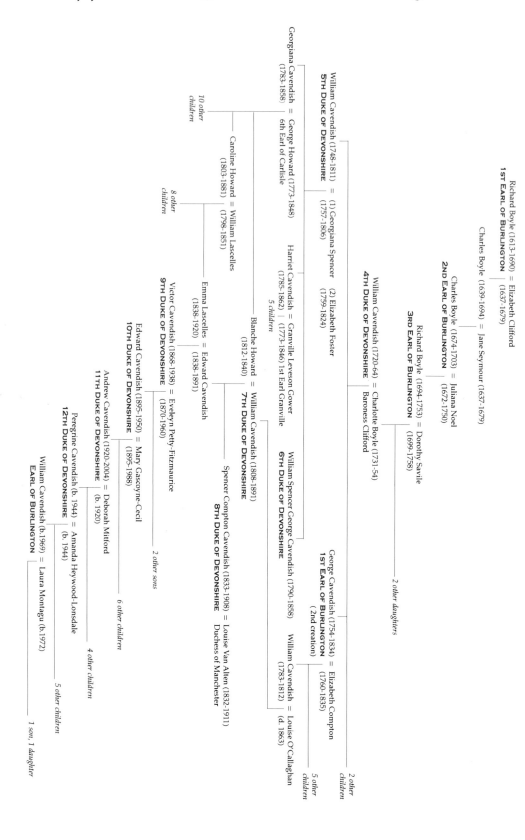

Appendix III

STRUCTURES IN CHISWICK HOUSE GROUNDS

With details of those included in English Heritage's *Statutory List of Buildings of Special Architectural or Historic Interest.*

*= in the care of English Heritage; other structures are owned by the London Borough of Hounslow, the majority of which are cared for by the Chiswick House and Gardens Trust on the Council's behalf. Responsibility will eventually be transferred to the Trust.

Listed Grade I

Chiswick House *
The Ionic Temple *
The Obelisk in the Orange Tree Garden *
The Doric Column *
Inigo Jones Gateway *
The Cascade and bridge over the Lake *
The Deer House *
The Classic Bridge *
The Obelisk at Burlington Lane Gate *
The Rustic House *
Burlington Lane Gates, piers and flanking walls *
Conservatory
Piers to the Forecourt
Statues of Inigo Jones and Andrea Palladio *
Urns, sphinxes, lion, lioness, 4 terms, 4 large urns lining avenue to rear of house
Three male statues in Classical togas (now inside the house)
Ten terms with female heads in semi-circle before front of the house

Listed Grade II

Duke's Avenue entrance gates and flanking stone walls *
Octagonal stone pond
Coade stone urns (now inside Conservatory)
South Lodge
Gates, gate piers and walls to the Southern Walled Garden *

Not listed

Lilly's Tomb *
Corney Road Gateway flanking walls to gateway and lamp standards*
Rustic Bridge *
Pedimented doorway to Hockey Field and flanking walls *
Rustic Arch (now Rustic Gate)
Brass sundial (modern)
Eyecatcher
Pebbled floor of Orangery *
Statue of Venus de Medici on Doric Column (put up 2009)
Sphinxes on Forecourt piers (replicas put up 2006)
Statue of Lion and Lioness on Staveley Road Gates
Two Coade Stone vases in Italian Garden (replicas)
Statue of `Ishmael in the Wilderness' in the Conservatory
Roman male figures in Exedra (replicas)
Lead Sphinx
Statue of `Nymph Bathing'
Plinth and vase by east end of Conservatory
`Stag' railing running from Inigo Jones Gateway to Summer Parlour *
Stone plinth near approach to House Forecourt
Staveley Road Gates and piers
Gate from Northern Walled Garden to car park *
Gates and piers at the A316 entrance
Gates and piers to Italian Garden from service yard *
Gate piers to service yard off Duke's Avenue *
Western gate to North Walled Garden
Arched opening between North and South Walled Gardens
Western gate to Southern Walled Garden
Eastern gate to Southern Walled Garden
Park Road Gates
Paxton House
Kent House
North Lodge
Cricket Pavilion
Learning Centre
Volunteer Building
Storage Barn
Café
Duke's Avenue lavatory block
Staveley Road lavatory block

SOURCES

Unpublished

Archive of the Chiswick House and Gardens Trust: reports and articles

Devonshire Archive, Chatsworth

Local Studies Collection, Chiswick Library: *Churchwardens Rates and Accounts 1622-1693; Borough of Brentford and Chiswick Council: Minutes of the Parks and Open Spaces Committee, 1929-1965*

Travers Morgan Planning for the Department of the Environment Directorate of Ancient Monuments and Historic Buildings *Chiswick House Grounds 1983*

English Heritage *Chiswick House and Grounds the Evolution of the buildings of Chiswick House and Associated Studies, nd*

Published

Barnard, Toby & Clark, Jane (eds) *Lord Burlington Art, Architecture and Life*, The Hambledon Press, 1995

Bessborough, Earl of (ed) *Georgiana: Extracts from the Correspondence of Georgiana, Duchess of Devonshire*, John Murray 1955

Clegg, Gillian *The Chiswick Book past and present*, Historical Publications Ltd, 2004

Draper, Warwick *Chiswick*, (1925) 1973 edition, Anne Bingley

Faulkner, Thomas *The History and Antiquities of Brentford, Ealing and Chiswick* , Simpkin, Marshall & Co, 1845

Foreman, Amanda *Georgiana Duchess of Devonshire*, Harper Collins, 1999

Harris, John *The Palladian Revival Lord Burlington, His Villa and Gardens at Chiswick*, Yale University Press, 1994

Lees-Milne, James *Earls of Creation*, Penguin 1962

Leveson Gower, Sir George & Palmer, Iris (eds) *Hary-O: The Letters of Lady Harriet Cavendish 1796-1809*, John Murray 1948

Masters, Brian *Georgiana Duchess of Devonshire*, Hamish Hamilton 1981

Victoria County History of the County of Middlesex vol VII, 1982

Websites

Chiswick House and Gardens Trust www.chgt.org.uk

English Heritage www.english-heritage.org.uk/chiswickhouse

Chiswick House Friends www.chfriends.org.uk

Chatsworth www.chatsworth.org

Gillian Clegg's Chiswick website www.chiswickhistory.org.uk

ILLUSTRATIONS

The author is grateful to English Heritage for permission to take photogaphs inside Chiswick House and to the other organisations and individuals for the use of their pictures. In some cases it was not possible to identify or contact the owner of the illustration so the author apologises if any copyrights have been infringed.

Back Cover Illustration, Chiswick House from the front (© Adam Watson)

INDEX